Selected Essays

By

Søren A. Kierkegaard

Translated by Charles K. Bellinger & L. M. Hollander

© 2011 Benediction Classics, Oxford.

Selected Essays by Kierkegaard

Søren Kierkegaard (1813 – 1855) was a prominent Danish Christian philosopher. This book contains a collection that is varied in theme and a good representation of Kierkegaard's literature. Readers will find his philosophy thought-provoking and meticulously well thought through. The essays included are:

- **'The Crowd Is Untruth'**
- **'Diapsalmata'**
- **'In Vino Veritas (The Banquet)'**
- **'Fear And Trembling'**
- **'Preparation For A Christian Life'**
- **Selections from 'The Present Moment'**

Contents

The Crowd Is Untruth 1
Diapsalmata 9
In Vino Veritas (The Banquet) 13
    (THE YOUNG PERSON'S SPEECH) 22
    (CONSTANTIN'S SPEECH) 37
    (VICTOR EREMITA'S SPEECH) 45
    (THE DRESSMAKER'S SPEECH) 54
Fear and Trembling 76
    INTRODUCTION 76
    PREPARATION 77
    I. 78
    II. 79
    III. 79
    IV. 80
    A PANEGYRIC ON ABRAHAM 81
    PRELIMINARY EXPECTORATION 88
Preparation for a Christian Life 103
    PART I 103
        I 103
        II 107
        III 111
        THE PAUSE 112
    PART II 125
        THE FIRST PHASE OF HIS LIFE 128
        THE SECOND PHASE OF HIS LIFE 140

PART III 144
    THE INVITATION AND THE INVITER 144
    CHRISTIANITY AS THE ABSOLUTE;
    CONTEMPORANEOUSNESS WITH CHRIST 148
    THE MORAL 153

Selections from 'The Present Moment' 155

    BY WAY OF INTRODUCTION 155
    A PANEGYRIC ON THE HUMAN RACE OR
    PROOF THAT THE NEW TESTAMENT IS NO
    LONGER TRUE 157
    IF WE ARE REALLY CHRISTIANS - THEN
    WHAT IS GOD? 159
    DIAGNOSIS 161
    THE CHRISTIANITY OF THE NEW
    TESTAMENT; 164
    THE CHRISTANITY OF "CHRISTENDOM" 164
    MODERN RELIGIOUS GUARANTEES 166
    WHAT SAYS THE FIRE-MARSHAL 168
    CONFIRMATION AND WEDDING
    CEREMONY; CHRISTIAN COMEDY-OR
    WORSE STILL 172
    THE WEDDING CEREMONY 175
    AN ETERNITY TO REPENT IN! 178
    A DOSE OF DISGUST WITH LIFE 180

The Crowd Is Untruth

On the Dedication to "That Single Individual" [1]

My dear, accept this dedication; it is given over, as it were, blindfolded, but therefore undisturbed by any consideration, in sincerity. Who you are, I know not; where you are, I know not; what your name is, I know not. Yet you are my hope, my joy, my pride, and my unknown honor.

It comforts me, that the right occasion is now there for you; which I have honestly intended during my labor and in my labor. For if it were possible that reading what I write became worldly custom, or even to give oneself out as having read it, in the hope of thereby winning something in the world, that then would not be the right occasion, since, on the contrary, misunderstanding would have triumphed, and it would have also deceived me, if I had not striven to prevent such a thing from happening.

This, in part, is a possible change in me, something I even wish for, basically a mood of soul and mind, which does not produce change by being more than change and therefore produces nothing less than change; it is rather an admission, in part a thoroughly and well thought-out view of "life," of "the truth," and of "the way."

---

[1] This, which is now considerably revised and enlarged, was written and intended to accompany the dedication to "that single individual," which is found in "Upbuilding Discourses in Various Spirits." Copenhagen, Spring 1847.

There is a view of life which holds that where the crowd is, the truth is also, that it is a need in truth itself, that it must have the crowd on its side.[1] There is another view of life; which holds that wherever the crowd is, there is untruth, so that, for a moment to carry the matter out to its farthest conclusion, even if every individual possessed the truth in private, yet if they came together into a crowd (so that "the crowd" received any *decisive*, voting, noisy, audible importance), untruth would at once be let in.[2]

For "the crowd" is untruth. Eternally, godly, christianly what Paul says is valid: "only one receives the prize," [I Cor. 9:24] not by way of comparison, for in the comparison "the others" are still present. That is to say, everyone can be that one, with God's help - but only one receives the prize; again, that is to say, everyone should cautiously have dealings with "the others," and essentially only talk with God and with himself - for only one receives the prize; again, that is to say, the human being is in kinship with, or to be a human is to be in kinship with the divinity. The worldly, temporal, busy, socially-friendly person says this: "How unreasonable, that only one should receive the prize, it is far more probable that several combined receive the prize; and if we become many, then it becomes more certain and also easier for each individually." Certainly, it is far *more probable*; and it is also true in relation to all earthly and sensuous prizes; and it becomes the only truth, if it is allowed to rule, for this point of view abolishes both God and the eternal and "the human being's" kinship with the divinity; it

---

[1] Perhaps, however, it is right to note once and for all, that which follows of itself and which I have never denied, that in relation to all temporal, earthly, worldly ends the crowd can have its validity, even its validity as a decisive court of last resort. But I am not speaking about such things, which I pay so little attention to. I speak of the ethical, the ethical-religious, of "the truth," and seen ethico-religiously the crowd is untruth, when it is taken as a valid court of last resort for what "the truth" is.

[2] Perhaps, however, it is right to note, although it seems to me to be almost superfluous, that it naturally could not occur to me to object to something, for example that there is preaching, or that "the truth" is proclaimed, even though it was to an assembly of a hundred thousand. No, but even if it were an assembly of just ten - and if there should be balloting, that is, if the assembly were the court of last resort, if the crowd were the decisive factor, then there <i>is</i> untruth.

abolishes it or changes it into a fable, and sets the modern (as a matter of fact, the old heathen) in its place, so that to be a human being is like being a specimen which belongs to a race gifted with reason, so that the race, the species, is higher than the individual, or so that there are only specimens, not individuals. But the eternal, which vaults high over the temporal, quiet as the night sky, and God in heaven, who from this exalted state of bliss, without becoming the least bit dizzy, looks out over these innumerable millions and knows each single individual; he, the great examiner, he says: only one receives the prize; that is to say, everyone can receive it, and everyone ought to become this by oneself, but only one receives the prize. Where the crowd is, therefore, or where a decisive importance is attached to the fact that there is a crowd, *there* no one is working, living, and striving for the highest end, but only for this or that earthly end; since the eternal, the decisive, can only be worked for where there is one; and to become this by oneself, which all can do, is to will to allow God to help you - "the crowd" is untruth.

A crowd - not this or that, one now living or long dead, a crowd of the lowly or of nobles, of rich or poor, etc., but in its very concept [1] - is untruth, since a crowd either renders the single individual wholly unrepentant and irresponsible, or weakens his responsibility by making it a fraction of his decision. Observe, there was not a single soldier who dared lay a hand on Caius Marius; this was the truth. But given three or four women with the consciousness or idea of being a crowd, with a certain hope in the possibility that no one could definitely say who it was or who started it: then they had the courage for it; what untruth! The untruth is first that it is "the crowd," which does either what only *the single individual* in the crowd does, or in every case what *each single individual* does. For a crowd is an abstraction, which does not have hands; each single individual, on the other hand, normally has two hands, and when he, as a single individual, lays his two

---

[1] The reader will therefore recall, that here by "crowd," "the crowd" is understood as a purely formal conceptual definition, not what one otherwise understands by "the crowd," when it supposedly is also a qualification, when human selfishness irreligiously divides human beings into "the crowd" and the nobles, and so forth. God in heaven, how would the religious arrive at such in-human equality! No, "crowd" is the number, the numerical; a number of noblemen, millionaires, high dignitaries, etc. - as soon as the numerical is at work, the "crowd" is "the crowd."

hands on Caius Marius, then it is the two hands of this single individual, not after all his neighbor's, even less - the crowd's, which has no hands. In the next place, the untruth is that the crowd had "the courage" for it, since never at any time was even the most cowardly of all single individuals so cowardly, as the crowd always is. For every single individual who escapes into the crowd, and thus flees in cowardice from being a single individual (who either had the courage to lay his hand on Caius Marius, or the courage to admit that he did not have it), contributes his share of cowardice to "the cowardice," which is: the crowd. Take the highest, think of Christ - and the whole human race, all human beings, which were ever born and ever will be born; the situation is the single individual, as an individual, in solitary surroundings alone with him; as a single individual he walks up to him and spits on him: the human being has never been born and never will be, who would have the courage or the impudence for it; this is the truth. But since they remain in a crowd, they have the courage for it - what frightening untruth.

The crowd is untruth. There is therefore no one who has more contempt for what it is to be a human being than those who make it their profession to lead the crowd. Let someone, some individual human being, certainly, approach such a person, what does he care about him; that is much too small a thing; he proudly sends him away; there must be at least a hundred. And if there are thousands, then he bends before the crowd, he bows and scrapes; what untruth! No, when there is an individual human being, then one should express the truth by respecting what it is to be a human being; and if perhaps, as one cruelly says, it was a poor, needy human being, then especially should one invite him into the best room, and if one has several voices, he should use the kindest and friendliest; that is the truth. When on the other hand it was an assembly of thousands or more, and "the truth" became the object of balloting, then especially one should godfearingly - if one prefers not to repeat in silence the Our Father: deliver us from evil - one should godfearingly express, that a crowd, as the court of last resort, ethically and religiously, is the untruth, whereas it is eternally true, that everyone can be the one. This is the truth.

The crowd is untruth. Therefore was Christ crucified, because he, even though he addressed himself to all, would not have to do with the crowd, because he would not in any way let a crowd help him, because he in this respect absolutely pushed away, would not found a party, or allow balloting, but would be what he was, the truth, which relates itself to the single individual. And therefore everyone who in truth will serve the truth, is *eo ipso* in some way or other a martyr; if it were possible that a human being in his mother's womb could make a decision to will to serve "the truth" in truth, so he also is *eo ipso* a martyr, however his martyrdom comes about, even while in his mother's womb. For to win a crowd is not so great a trick; one only needs some talent, a certain dose of untruth and a little acquaintance with the human passions. But no witness for the truth - alas, and every human being, you and I, should be one - dares have dealings with a crowd. The witness for the truth - who naturally will have nothing to do with politics, and to the utmost of his ability is careful not to be confused with a politician - the godfearing work of the witness to the truth is to have dealings with all, if possible, but always individually, to talk with each privately, on the streets and lanes - to split up the crowd, or to talk to it, not to form a crowd, but so that one or another individual might go home from the assembly and become a single individual. "A crowd," on the other hand, when it is treated as the court of last resort in relation to "the truth," its judgment as *the* judgment, is detested by the witness to the truth, more than a virtuous young woman detests the dance hall. And they who address the "crowd" as the court of last resort, he considers to be instruments of untruth. For to repeat: that which in politics and similar domains has its validity, sometimes wholly, sometimes in part, becomes untruth, when it is transferred to the intellectual, spiritual, and religious domains. And at the risk of a possibly exaggerated caution, I add just this: by "truth" I always understand "eternal truth." But politics and the like has nothing to do with "eternal truth." A politics, which in the real sense of "eternal truth" made a serious effort to bring "eternal truth" into real life, would in the same second show itself to be in the highest degree the most "impolitic" thing imaginable.

The crowd is untruth. And I could weep, in every case I can learn to long for the eternal, whenever I think about our age's misery, even compared with the ancient world's greatest misery, in that the daily press and anonymity make our age even more insane with help from "the public," which is really an abstraction, which makes a claim to be the court of last resort in relation to "the truth"; for assemblies which make this claim surely do not take place. That an anonymous person, with help from the press, day in and day out can speak however he pleases (even with respect to the intellectual, the ethical, the religious), things which he perhaps did not in the least have the courage to say personally in a particular situation; every time he opens up his gullet - one cannot call it a mouth - he can *all at once* address himself to thousands upon thousands; he can get ten thousand times ten thousand to repeat after him - and no one has to answer for it; in ancient times the relatively unrepentant crowd was the almighty, but now there is the absolutely unrepentant thing: No One, an anonymous person: the Author, an anonymous person: the Public, sometimes even anonymous subscribers, therefore: No One. No One! God in heaven, such states even call themselves Christian states. One cannot say that, again with the help of the press, "the truth" can overcome the lie and the error. O, you who say this, ask yourself: Do you dare to claim that human beings, in a crowd, are just as quick to reach for truth, which is not always palatable, as for untruth, which is always deliciously prepared, when in addition this must be combined with an admission that one has let oneself be deceived! Or do you dare to claim that "the truth" is just as quick to let itself be understood as is untruth, which requires no previous knowledge, no schooling, no discipline, no abstinence, no self-denial, no honest self-concern, no patient labor! No, "the truth," which detests this untruth, the only goal of which is to desire its increase, is not so quick on its feet. Firstly, it cannot work through the fantastical, which is the untruth; its communicator is only a single individual. And its communication relates itself once again to the single individual; for in this view of life the single individual is precisely the truth. The truth can neither be communicated nor be received without being as it were before the eyes of God, nor without God's help, nor without God being involved as the middle term, since he is the truth. It can therefore only be communicated by and received by "the single individual," which, for that matter, every single human being who lives could be: this is the determination of the truth in contrast to the abstract, the fantastical, impersonal, "the crowd" - "the public," which excludes God as the middle term (for the *personal* God cannot be the middle term in an *impersonal* relation), and also thereby the truth, for God is the truth and its middle term.

And to honor every individual human being, unconditionally every human being, that is the truth and fear of God and love of "the neighbor"; but ethico-religiously viewed, to recognize "the crowd" as the court of last resort in relation to "the truth," that is to deny God and cannot possibly be to love "the neighbor." And "the neighbor" is the absolutely true expression for human equality; if everyone in truth loved the neighbor as himself, then would perfect human equality be unconditionally attained; everyone who in truth loves the neighbor, expresses unconditional human equality; everyone who is really aware (even if he admits, like I, that his effort is weak and imperfect) that the task is to love the neighbor, he is also aware of what human equality is. But never have I read in the Holy Scriptures this command: You shall love the crowd; even less: You shall, ethico-religiously, recognize in the crowd the court of last resort in relation to "the truth." It is clear that to love the neighbor is self-denial, that to love the crowd or to act as if one loved it, to make it the court of last resort for "the truth," that is the way to truly gain power, the way to all sorts of temporal and worldly advantage - yet it is untruth; for the crowd is untruth.

But he who acknowledges this view, which is seldom presented (for it often happens, that a man believes that the crowd is in untruth, but when it, the crowd, merely accepts his opinion *en masse*, then everything is all right), he admits to himself that he is the weak and powerless one; how would a single individual be able to stand against the many, who have the power! And he could not then want to get the crowd on his side to carry through the view that the crowd, ethico-religiously, as the court of last resort, is untruth; that would be to mock himself. But although this view was from the first an admission of weakness and powerlessness, and since it seems therefore so uninviting, and is therefore heard so seldom: yet it has the good feature, that it is fair, that it offends no one, not a single one, that it does not distinguish between persons, not a single one. A crowd is indeed made up of single individuals; it must therefore be in everyone's power to become what he is, a single individual; no one is prevented from being a single individual, no one, unless he prevents himself by becoming many. To become a crowd, to gather a crowd around oneself, is on the contrary to distinguish life from life; even the most well-meaning one who talks about that, can easily offend a single individual. But it is the crowd which has power, influence, reputation, and domination - this is the distinction of life from life, which tyrannically overlooks the single individual as the weak and powerless one, in a temporal-worldly way overlooks the eternal truth: the single individual.

Note The reader will recall, that this (the beginning of which is marked by the atmosphere of its moment, when I voluntarily exposed myself to the brutality of literary vulgarity) was originally written in 1846, although later revised and considerably enlarged. Existence, almighty as it is, has since that time shed light on the proposition that the crowd, seen ethico-religiously as the court of last resort, is untruth. Truly, I am well served by this; I am even helped by it to better understand myself, since I will now be understood in a completely different way than I was at the time, when my weak, lonely voice was heard as a ridiculous exaggeration, whereas it can now scarcely be heard at all on account of existence's loud voice, which says the same thing,

Diapsalmata[1]

What is a poet? An unhappy man who conceals profound anguish in his heart, but whose lips are so fashioned that when sighs and groans pass over them they sound like beautiful music. His fate resembles that of the unhappy men who were slowly roasted by a gentle fire in the tyrant Phalaris' bull—their shrieks could not reach his ear to terrify him, to him they sounded like sweet music. And people flock about the poet and say to him: do sing again; which means, would that new sufferings tormented your soul, and: would that your lips stayed fashioned as before, for your cries would only terrify us, but your music is delightful. And the critics join them, saying: well done, thus must it be according to the laws of aesthetics. Why, to be sure, a critic resembles a poet as one pea another, the only difference being that he has no anguish in his heart and no music on his lips. Behold, therefore would I rather be a swineherd on Amager[2], and be understood by the swine than a poet, and misunderstood by men.

In addition to my numerous other acquaintances I have still one more intimate friend—my melancholy. In the midst of pleasure, in the midst of work, he beckons to me, calls me aside, even though I remain present bodily. My melancholy is the most faithful sweetheart I have had—no wonder that I return the love!

---

[1] Interlude (of aphorisms). Selection
[2] A flat island south of the capital, called the "Kitchen Garden of -Copenhagen."

Of all ridiculous things the most ridiculous seems to me, to be busy—to be a man who is brisk about his food and his work. Therefore, whenever I see a fly settling, in the decisive moment, on the nose of such a person of affairs; or if he is spattered with mud from a carriage which drives past him in still greater haste; or the drawbridge opens up before him; or a tile falls down and knocks him dead, then I laugh heartily. And who, indeed, could help laughing? What, I wonder, do these busy folks get done? Are they not to be classed with the woman who in her confusion about the house being on fire carried out the firetongs? What things of greater account, do you suppose, will they rescue from life's great conflagration?

Let others complain that the times are wicked. I complain that they are paltry; for they are without passion. The thoughts of men are thin and frail like lace, and they themselves are feeble like girl lace-makers. The thoughts of their hearts are too puny to be sinful. For a worm it might conceivably be regarded a sin to harbor thoughts such as theirs, not for a man who is formed in the image of God. Their lusts are staid and sluggish, their passions sleepy; they do their duty, these sordid minds, but permit themselves, as did the Jews, to trim the coins just the least little bit, thinking that if our Lord keep tab of them ever so carefully one might yet safely venture to fool him a bit. Fye upon them! It is therefore my soul ever returns to the Old Testament and to Shakespeare. There at least one feels that one is dealing with men and women; there one hates and loves, there one murders one's enemy and curses his issue through all generations—there one sins.

Just as, according to the legend[1] Parmeniscus in the Trophonian cave lost his ability to laugh, but recovered it again on the island of Delos at the sight of a shapeless block which was exhibited as the image of the goddess Leto: likewise did it happen to me. When I was very young I forgot in the Trophonian cave how to laugh; but when I grew older and opened my eyes and contemplated the real world, I had to laugh, and have not ceased laughing, ever since. I beheld that the meaning of life was to make a living; its goal, to become Chief Justice; that the delights of love consisted in marrying a woman with ample means; that it was the blessedness of friendship to help one another in financial difficulties; that wisdom was what most people supposed it to

---

[1] Told by Athenaios.

be; that it showed enthusiasm to make a speech, and courage, to risk being fined 10 dollars; that it was cordiality to say "may it agree with you" after a repast; that it showed piety to partake of the communion once a year. Saw that and laughed.

A strange thing happened to me in my dream. I was rapt into the Seventh Heaven. There sat all the gods assembled. As a special dispensation I was granted the favor to have one wish. "Do you wish for youth," said Mercury, "or for beauty, or power, or a long life; or do you wish for the most beautiful woman, or any other of the many fine things we have in our treasure trove? Choose, but only one thing!" For a moment I was at a loss. Then I addressed the gods in this wise: "Most honorable contemporaries, I choose one thing—that I may always have the laughs on MY side." Not one god made answer, but all began to laugh. From this I concluded that my wish had been granted and thought that the gods knew how to express themselves with good taste: for it would surely have been inappropriate to answer gravely: your wish has been granted.

In Vino Veritas (The Banquet)

It was on one of the last days in July, at ten o'clock in the evening, when the participants in that banquet assembled together. Date and year I have forgotten; indeed this would be interesting only to one's memory of details: and not to one's recollection of the contents of what experience. The "spirit of the occasion" and whatever impressions are recorded in one's mind under that heading, concerns only one's recollections; and just as generous wine gains in flavor by passing the Equator, because of the evaporation of its watery particles, likewise does recollection gain by getting rid of the watery particles of memory; and yet recollection becomes as little a mere figment of the imagination by this process as does the generous wine.
The participants were five in number: John, with the epithet of the Seducer, Victor Eremita, Constantin Constantius, and yet two others whose names I have not exactly forgotten--which would be a matter of small importance but whose names I did not learn. It was as if these two had no proper names, for they were constantly addressed by some epithet. The one was called the Young Person. Nor was he more than twenty and some years, of slender and delicate build, and of a very dark complexion. His face was thoughtful; but more pleasing even was its lovable and engaging expression which betokened a purity of soul harmonizing perfectly with the soft charm, almost feminine, and the transparency of his whole presence. This external beauty of appearance was lost sight of, however, in one's next impression of him; or, one kept it only in mind whilst regarding a youth nurtured orto use a still tenderer expression--petted into being, by thought, and nourished by the contents of his own soul a youth who as yet had had nothing to do with the world, had been neither aroused and fired, nor disquieted and disturbed. Like a sleep-walker he bore the law of his actions with-

in himself, and the amiable, kindly expression of his countenance concerned no one, but only mirrored the disposition of his soul.

The other person they called the Dressmaker, and that was his occupation. Of him it was impossible to get a consistent impression. He was dressed according to the very latest fashion, with his hair curled and perfumed, fragrant with eau-de-cologne. One moment his carriage did not lack self-possession, whereas in the next it assumed a certain festive air, a certain hovering motion which, however was kept in rather definite bounds by the robustness of his figure. Even when he was most malicious in his speech his voice ever had a touch of the smooth-tonguedness of the shop, the suaveness of the dealer in fancy-goods, Which evidently was utterly disgusting to himself and only satisfied his spirit of defiance. As I think of him now I understand him better, to be sure, than when I first saw him step out of his carriage and I involuntarily laughed. At the same time there is some contradiction left still. He had transformed or bewitched himself, had by the magic of his own will assumed the appearance of one almost half-witted, but had not thereby entirely satisfied himself; and this is why his reflectiveness now and then peered forth from beneath his disguise.

As I think of it now it seems rather absurd that five such persons should get a banquet arranged. Nor would anything have come of it, I suppose, if Constantin had not been one of us. In a retired room of a confectioner's shop where they met at times, the matter had been broached once before, but had been dropped immediately when the question arose as to who was to head the undertaking. The Young Person was declared unfit for that task, the Dressmaker affirmed himself to be too busy. Victor Eremita did not beg to be excused because "he had married a wife or bought yoke of oxen which he needed to prove",[1] but, he said, even if he should make an exception, for once, and come to the banquet, yet he would decline the courtesy offered him to preside at it, and he therewith "entered protest at the proper time.[2] This, John considered a work spoken in due season; because, as he saw it, there was but one person able to prepare a banquet, and that was the possessor of the wishing-table which set itself with delectable things whenever he said to it "Cover thyself!" He averred that to enjoy the charms of a young girl in haste was not always the wisest course; but as to a banquet, he would not wait for it, and generally was tired of

---

[1] Cf. Luke XIV, 19-20.
[2] Words used in the banns.

it a long while before it came off. However, if the plan was to be carried into effect he would make one condition, which was, that the banquet should be so arranged as to be served in one course. And that all were agreed on. Also, that the settings for it were to be made altogether new, and that afterwards they were to be destroyed entirely; ay, before rising from table one was to hear the preparation for their destruction. Nothing was to remain; "not even so much," said the Dressmaker, "as there is left of a dress after it has been made over into a hat." "Nothing," said John, "because nothing is more unpleasant than a sentimental scene, and nothing more disgusting than the knowledge that somewhere or other there is an external setting which in a direct and impertinent fashion pretends to be a reality."

When the conversation had thus become animated, Victor Eremita suddenly arose, struck an attitude on the floor, beckoned with his hand in the fashion of one commanding and, holding his arm extended as one lifting a goblet, he said, with the gesture of one waving a welcome: "With this cup whose fragrance already intoxicates my senses, whose cool fire already inflames my blood, I greet you, beloved fellow-banqueters, and bid you welcome; being entirely assured that each one of you is sufficiently satisfied by our merely speaking about the banquet; for our Lord satisfied the stomach before satisfying the eye, but the imagination acts in the reverse fashion." Thereupon he inserted his hand in his pocket, took from it a cigar-case, struck a match, and began to smoke. When Constantin Constantius protested against this sovereign free way of transforming the banquet planned into an illusory fragment of life, Victor declared that he did not believe for one moment that such a banquet could be got up and that, in any case, it had been a mistake to let it become the subject of discussion in advance. "Whatever is to be good must come at once; for 'at once' is the divinest of all categories and deserves to be honored as in the language of the Romans: ex templo,[1] because it is the starting point for all that is divine in life, and so much so that what is not done at once is of evil." However, he remarked, he did not care to argue this point. In case the others wished to speak and act differently he would not say a word, but if they wished him to explain the sense of his remarks more fully he must have leave to make a speech, because he did not consider it all desirable to provoke a discussion on the subject.

---

[1] Which in Latin means both "from the temple" and "at once."

Permission was given him; and as the others called on him to do so at once, he spoke as follows: "A banquet is in itself a difficult matter, because even if it be arranged with ever so much taste and talent there is something else essential to its success, to-wit, good luck. And by this I mean not such matters as most likely would give concern to an anxious hostess, but something different, a something which no one can make absolutely sure of: a fortunate harmonizing of the spirit and the minutiae of the banquet, that fine ethereal vibration of chords, that soul-stirring music which cannot be ordered in advance from the town-musicians. Look you, therefore is it a hazardous thing to undertake, because if things do go wrong, perhaps from the very start, one may suffer such a depression and loss of spirits that recovery from it might involve a very long time.

"Sheer habit and thoughtlessness are father and godfather to most banquets, and it is only due to the lack of critical sense among people that one fails to notice the utter absence of any idea in them. In the first place, women ought never to be present at a banquet. Women may be used to advantage only in the Greek style, as a chorus of dancers. As it is the main thing at a banquet that there be eating and drinking, woman ought not to be present; she cannot do justice to what is offered; or, if she can, it is most unbeautiful. Whenever a woman is present the matter of eating and drinking ought to be reduced to the very slightest proportions. At most, it ought to be no more than some trifling feminine occupation, to have something to busy one's hands with. Especially in the country a little repast of this kind which, by the way, should be put at other times than the principal meals--may be extremely delightful; and if so, always owing to the presence of the other sex. To do like the English, who let the fair sex retire as soon as the real drinking is to start, is to fall between two stools, for every plan ought to be a whole, and the very manner with which I take a seat at the table and seize hold of knife and fork bears a definite relation to this whole. In the same sense a political banquet presents an unbeautiful ambiguity inasmuch as one does not[1] want to cut down to a very minimum the essentials of a banquet, and yet does not wish to have the speeches thought of as having been made over the cups.

"So far, we are agreed, I suppose; and our number in case anything should come of the banquet--is correctly chosen, according to that

---

[1] The omission of the negative particle in the original is no doubt unintentional.

beautiful rule: neither more than the Muses nor fewer than the Graces. Now I demand the greatest superabundance of everything thinkable. That is, even though everything be not actually there, yet the possibility of having it must be at one's immediate beck and call, aye, hover temptingly over the table, more seductive even than the actual sight of it. I beg to be excused, however, from banqueting on sulphur-matches or on a piece of sugar which all are to suck in turn. My demands for such a banquet will, on the contrary, be difficult to satisfy; for the feast itself must be calculated to arouse and incite that unmentionable longing which each worthy participant is to bring with him. I require that the earth's fertility be at our service, as though everything sprouted forth at the very moment the desire for it was born. I desire a more luxurious abundance of wine than when Mephistopheles needed but to drill holes into the table to obtain it. I demand an illumination more splendid than have the gnomes when they lift up the mountain on pillars and dance in a sea of blazing light. I demand what most excites the senses, I demand their gratification by deliciously sweet perfumes, more superb than any in the Arabian Nights. I demand a coolness which voluptuously provokes desire and breathes relaxation on desire satisfied. I demand a fountain's unceasing enlivenment. If Maecenas could not sleep without hearing the splashing of a fountain, I cannot eat without it. Do not misunderstand me, I can eat stockfish without it; but I cannot eat at a banquet without it; I can drink water without it, but I cannot drink wine at a banquet without it. I demand a host of servants, chosen and comely, as if I sat at table with the gods; I demand that there shall be music at the feast, both strong and subdued; and I demand that it shall be an accompaniment to my thoughts; and what concerns you, my friends, my demands regarding you are altogether incredible. Do you see, by reason of all these demands--which are as many reasons against it I hold a banquet to be a pium desideratum,[1] and am so far from desiring a repetition of it that I presume it is not feasible even a first time."

The only one who had not actually participated in this conversation, nor in the frustration of the banquet, was Constantin. Without him, nothing would have been done save the talking. He had come to a different conclusion and was of the opinion that the idea might well be realized, if one but carried the matter with a high hand.

---

[1] Pious wish.

Then some time passed, and both the banquet and the discussion about it were forgotten, when suddenly, one day, the participants received a card of invitation from Constantius for a banquet the very same evening. The motto of the Party had been given by him as: In Vino Veritas, because there was to be speaking, to be sure, and not only conversation; but the speeches were not to be made except in vino, and no truth was to be uttered there excepting that which is in vino--when the wine is a defense of the truth and the truth a defense of the wine.

The place had been chosen in the woods, some ten miles distant from Copenhagen. The hall in which they were to feast had been newly decorated and in every way made unrecognizable; a smaller room, separated from the hall by a corridor, was arranged for an orchestra. Shutters and curtains were let down before all windows, which were left open. The arrangement that the participants were to drive to the banquet in the evening hour was to intimate to them and that was Constantin's idea what was to follow. Even if one knows that one is driving to a banquet, and the imagination therefore indulges for a moment in thoughts of luxury, yet the impression of the natural surroundings is too powerful to be resisted. That this might possibly not be the case was the only contingency he apprehended; for just as there is no power like the imagination to render beautiful all it touches, neither is there any power which can to such a degree disturb all misfortune conspiring if confronted with reality. But driving on a summer evening does not lure the imagination to luxurious thoughts, but rather to the opposite. Even if one does not see it or hear it, the imagination will unconsciously create a picture of the longing for home which one is apt to feel in the evening hours one sees the reapers, man and maid, returning from their work in the fields, one hears the hurried rattling of the hay wagon, one interprets even the far-away lowing from the meadows as a longing. Thus does a summer evening suggest idyllic thoughts, soothing even a restless mind with its assuagement, inducing even the soaring imagination to abide on earth with an indwelling yearning for home as the place from whence it came, and thus teaching the insatiable mind to be satisfied with little, by rendering one content; for in the evening hour time stands still and eternity lingers. Thus they arrived in the evening hour: those invited; for Constantin had come out somewhat earlier. Victor Eremita who resided in the country not far away came on horseback, the others in a carriage. And just as they had discharged it, a light open vehicle rolled in through the gate carrying a merry company of four journeymen who were entertained to be ready at the decisive moment to function as a corps of destruction: just as firemen are stationed in a theatre, for the opposite reason at once to extinguish a fire.

So long as one is a child one possesses sufficient imagination to maintain one's soul at the very top-notch of expectation--for a whole hour in the dark room, if need be; but when one has grown older one's imagination may easily cause one to tire of the Christmas tree before seeing it.

The folding doors were opened. The effect of the radiant illumination, the coolness wafting toward them, the beguiling fragrance of sweet perfumes, the excellent taste of the arrangements, for a moment overwhelmed the feelings of those entering; and when, at the same time, strains from the ballet of "Don Juan" sounded from the orchestra, their persons seemed transfigured and, as if out of reverence for an unseen spirit about them, they stopped short for a moment like men who have been roused by admiration and who have risen to admire.

Whoever knows that happy moment, whoever has appreciated its delight, and has not also felt the apprehension lest suddenly something might happen, some trifle perhaps, which yet might be sufficient to disturb all! Whoever has held the lamp of Aladdin in his hand and has not also felt the swooning of pleasure, because one needs but to wish? Whoever has held what is inviting in his hand and has not also learned to keep his wrist limber to let go at once, if need be?

Thus they stood side by side. Only Victor stood alone, absorbed in thought; a shudder seemed to pass through his soul, he almost trembled; he collected himself and saluted the omen with these words: "Ye mysterious, festive, and seductive strains which drew me out of the cloistered seclusion of a quiet youth and beguiled me with a longing as mighty as a recollection, and terrible, as though Elvira had not even been seduced but had only desired to be! Immortal Mozart, thou to whom I owe all; but no! As yet I do not owe thee all. But when I shall have become an old man if ever I do become an old man; or when I shall have become ten years older if ever I do; or when I am become old if ever I shall become old; or when I shall die for that, indeed, I know I shall: then shall I say: immortal Mozart, thou to whom I owe all and then I shall let my admiration, which is my soul's first and only admiration, burst forth in all its might and let it make away with me, as it often has been on the point of doing. Then have I set my house in order,[1] then have I remembered my beloved one, then have I confessed my love, then have I fully established that I owe thee all, then am I occupied no longer with thee, with the world, but only with the grave thought of death."

Now there came from the orchestra that invitation in which joy triumphs most exultantly, and heaven-storming soars aloft above Elvira's sorrowful thanks; and gracefully apostrophizing, John repeated: "Viva la liberta" "et veritas," said the Young Person; "but above all, in vino," Constantin interrupted them, seating himself at the table and inviting the others to do likewise.

How easy to prepare a banquet; yet Constantin declared that he never would risk preparing another. How easy to admire; yet Victor declared that he never again would lend words to his admiration; for to suffer a discomfiture is more dreadful than to become an invalid in war! How easy to express a desire, if one has the magic lamp; yet that is at times more terrible than to perish of want!

They were seated. In the same moment the little company were launched into the very middle of the infinite sea of enjoyment as if with one single bound. Each one had addressed all his thoughts and all his desires to the banquet, had prepared his soul for the enjoyment which was offered to overflowing and in which their souls overflowed. The experienced driver is known by his ability to start the snorting team with a single bound and to hold them well abreast; the well-trained steed is known by his lifting him-self in one absolutely decisive leap: even if one or the other of the guests perhaps fell short in some particular, cer-tainly Constantin was a good host.

Thus they banqueted. Soon, conversation had woven its beautiful wreaths about the banqueters, so that they sat garlanded. Now, it was enamored of the food, now of the wine, and now again of itself; now, it seemed to develop into significance, and then again it was altogether slight. Soon, fancy unfolded itself the splendid one which blows but once, the tender one which straightway closes its petals; now, there came an exclamation from one of the banqueters: "These truffles are superb," and now, an order of the host: "This Chateau Margaux!" Now, the music was drowned in the noise, now it was heard again. Sometimes the servants stood still as if in pausa, in that decisive moment when a new dish was being brought out, or a new wine was ordered and mentioned by name, sometimes they were all a-bustle.

---

[1] 2 Kings 20, 1; Isaiah 38,1.

Sometimes there was a silence for a moment, and then the re-animating spirit of the music went forth over the guests. Now, one with some bold thought would take the lead in the conversation and the others followed after, almost forgetting to eat, and the music would sound after them as it sounds after the jubilant shouts of a host storming on; now, only the clinking of glasses and the clattering of plates was heard and the feasting proceeded in silence, accompanied only by the music that joyously advanced and again stimulated conversation. Thus they banqueted.

How poor is language in comparison with that symphony of sounds unmeaning, yet how significant, whether of a battle or of a banquet, which even scenic representation cannot imitate and for which language has but a few words! How rich is language in the expression of the world of ideas, and how poor, when it is to describe reality!

Only once did Constantin abandon his omnipresence ill which one actually lost sight of his presence. At the very beginning he got them to sing one of the old drinking songs, "by way of calling to mind that jolly time when men and women feasted together," as he said a proposal which had the positively burlesque effect he had perhaps calculated it should have. It almost gained the upper hand when the Dressmaker wanted them to sing the ditty: "When I shall mount the bridal bed, hoiho!" After a couple of courses had been served Constantin proposed that the banquet should conclude with each one's making a speech, but that precautions should be taken against the speakers' divagating too much. He was for making two conditions, viz., there were to be no speeches until after the meal; and no one was to speak before having drunk sufficiently to feel the power of the wine else he was to be in that condition in which one says much which under other circumstances one would leave unsaid without necessarily having the connection of speech and thought constantly interrupted by hiccoughs.[1] Before speaking, then, each one was to declare solemnly that he was in that condition. No definite quantity of wine was to be required, capacities differed so widely. Against this proposal, John entered protest. He could never become intoxicated, he averred, and when he had come to a certain point he grew the soberer the more he drank. Victor Eremita was, of the opinion that any such preparatory premeditations to insure one's becoming drunk would precisely militate against one's becoming so. If one desired to become intoxicated

---

[1] An allusion to the plight of Aristophanes in Plato's Symposium.

the deliberate wish was only a hindrance. Then there ensued some discussion about the divers influences of wine on consciousness, and especially about the fact that, in the case of a reflective temperament, an excess of wine may manifest itself, not in any particular impetus but, on the contrary, in a noticeably cool self-possession. As to the contents of the speeches, Constantin proposed that they should deal with love, that is, the relation between man and woman. No love stories were to be told though they might furnish the text of one's remarks.

The conditions were accepted. All reasonable and just demands a host may make on his guests were fulfilled: they ate and drank, and "drank and were filled with drink," as the Bible has it;[1] that is, they drank stoutly.

The desert was served. Even if Victor had not, as yet, had his desire gratified to hear the splashing of a fountain, which, for that matter, he had luckily forgotten since that former conversation now champagne flowed profusely. The clock struck twelve. Thereupon Constantin commanded silence, saluted the Young Person with a goblet and the words quod felix sit faustumque[2] and bade him to speak first.

(The Young Person's Speech)

The Young Person arose and declared that he felt the power of the wine, which was indeed apparent to some degree; for the blood pulsed strongly in his temples, and his appearance was not as beautiful as before the meal. He spoke as follows:

If there be truth in the words of the poets, dear fellow banqueters, then unrequited love is, indeed, the greatest of sorrows. Should you require any proof of this you need but listen to the speech of lovers. They say that it is death, certain death; and the first time they believe it for the space of two weeks. The next time they say that it is death; and finally they will die sometime as the result of unrequited love. For that love has killed them, about that there can obtain no doubt. And as to love's having to take hold three times to make away with them, that is not different from the dentist's having to pull three times before he is able to budge that firmly rooted molar. But, if unrequited love thus

---

[1] Haggai 1, 6 (inexact).
[2] May it be fortunate and favorable.

means certain death, how happy am I who have never loved and, I hope, will only achieve dying some time, and not from unrequited love! But just this may be the greatest misfortune, for all I know, and how unfortunate must I then be!

The essence of love probably (for I speak as does a blind man about colors), probably lies in its bliss; which is, in other words, that the cessation of love brings death to the lover. This I comprehend very well as in the nature of a hypothesis correlating life and death. But, if love is to be merely by way of hypothesis, why, then lovers lay themselves open to ridicule through their actually falling in love. If, however, love is something real, why, then reality must bear out what lovers say about it. But did one in real life ever hear of, or observe, such things having taken place, even if there is hearsay to that effect? Here I perceive already one of the contradictions in which love involves a person; for whether this is different for those initiated, that I have no means of knowing; but love certainly does seem to involve people in the most curious contradictions.

There is no other relation between human beings which makes such demands on one's ideality as does love, and yet love is never seen to have it. For this reason alone I would be afraid of love; for I fear that it might have the power to make me too talk vaguely about a bliss which I did not feel and a sorrow I did not have. I say this here since I am bidden to speak on love, though unacquainted with it I say this in surroundings which appeal to me like a Greek symposium; for I should otherwise not care to speak on this subject as I do not wish to disturb any one's happiness but, rather, am content with my own thoughts. Who knows but these thoughts are sheer imbecilities and vain imaginings perhaps my ignorance is explicable from the fact that I never have learned, nor have wished to learn, from any one, how one comes to love; or from the fact that I have never yet challenged a woman with a glance which is supposed to be smart but have always lowered my eyes, unwilling to yield to an impression before having fully made sure about the nature of the power into whose sphere I am venturing.

At this point he was interrupted by Constantin who expostulated with him because, by his very confession of never having been in love, he had debarred himself from speaking. The Young Person declared that at any other time he would gladly obey an injunction to that effect as he had often enough experienced how tiresome it was to have to make a speech; but that in this case he would insist upon his right. Precisely the fact that one had had no love affair, he said, also constituted an affair of love; and he who could assert this of himself was entitled to speak about Eros just because his thoughts were bound to take issue with the whole sex and not with individuals. He was granted permission to speak and continued.

Inasmuch as my right to speak has been challenged, this may serve to exempt me from your laughter; for I know well that, just as among rustics he is not considered a man who does not call a tobacco pipe his own, likewise among men-folks he is not considered a real man who is not experienced in love. If any one feels like laughing, let him laugh my thought is, and remains, the essential consideration for me. Or is love, perchance, privileged to be the only event which is to be considered after, rather than before, it happens? If that be the case, what then if I, having fallen in love, should later on think that it was too late to think about it? Look you, this is the reason why I choose to think about love before it happens. To be sure, lovers also maintain that they gave the matter thought, but such is not the case. They assume it to be essential in man to fall in love; but this surely does not mean thinking about love but, rather, assuming it, in order to make sure of getting one's self a sweetheart.

In fact, whenever my reflection endeavors to pin down love, naught but contradiction seems to remain. At times, it is true, I feel as if something had escaped me, but I cannot tell what it is, whereas my reflection is able at once to point out the contradictions in what does occur. Very well, then, in my opinion love is the greatest self-contradiction imaginable, and comical at the same time. Indeed, the one corresponds to the other. The comical is always seen to occur in the category of contradictions which truth I cannot take the time to demonstrate now; but what I shall demonstrate now is that love is comical. By love I mean the relation between man and woman. I am not thinking of Eros in the Greek sense which has been extolled so beautifully by Plato who, by the way, is so far from considering the love of woman that he mentions it only in passing, holding it to be inferior to the love of youths.[1] I say, love is comical to a third person more I say not. Whether it is for this reason that lovers always hate a third person I do not know; but I do know that reflection is always in such a relation the third person, and for this reason I cannot love without at the same time having a third person present in the shape of my reflection.

---

[1] Symposium, ch.9.

Søren Kierkegaard

This surely cannot seem strange to anyone, every one having doubted everything, whereas I am uttering my doubts only with reference to love. And yet I do think it strange that people have doubted everything and have again reached certainty, without as much as dropping a word concerning the difficulties which have held my thought captive so much so that I have, now and then, longed to be freed of them freed by the aid of one, note well, who was aware of these difficulties, and not of one who in his sleep had a notion to doubt, and to have doubted, everything, and again in his sleep had the notion that he is explaining, and has explained, all.[1]

Let me then have your attention, dear fellow banqueters, and if you yourselves be lovers do not therefore interrupt me, nor try to silence me because you do not wish to hear the explanation. Rather turn away and listen with averted faces to what I have to say, and what I insist upon saying, having once begun.

In the first place I consider it comical that everyone loves, and every one wishes to love, without any one ever being able to tell one what is the nature of the lovable or that which is the real object of love. As to the word "to love" I shall not discuss it since it means nothing definite; but as soon as the matter is broached at all we are met by the question as to what it is one loves. No other answer is ever vouchsafed us on that point other than that one loves what is lovable. For if one should make answer, with Plato,[2] that one is to love what is good, one has in taking this single step exceeded the bounds of the erotic.

The answer may be offered, perhaps, that one is to love what is beautiful. But if I then should ask whether to love means to love a beautiful landscape or a beautiful painting it would be immediately perceived that the erotic is not, as it were, comprised in the more general term of the love of things beautiful, but is something entirely of its own kind. Were a lover just to give an example to speak as follows, in order to express adequately how much love there dwelled in him: "I love beautiful landscapes, and my Lalage, and the beautiful dancer, and a beautiful horse--in short, love all that is beautiful," his Lalage would not be satisfied with his encomium, however well satisfied she

---

[1] This ironic sally refers, not to Descartes' principle of skepsis, but to the numerous Danish followers of Hegel and his "method"; cf. Fear and Trembling, p. 119.
[2] Symposium, ch. 24.

might be with him in all other respects, and even if she be beautiful; and now suppose Lalage is not beautiful and he yet loved her!

Again, if I should refer the erotic element to the bisection of which Aristophanes tells us[1] when he says that the gods severed man into two parts as one cuts flounders, and that these parts thus separated sought one another, then I again encounter a difficulty I cannot get over, which is, in how far I may base my reasoning on Aristophanes who in his speech just because there is no reason for the thought to stop at this point--goes further in his thought and thinks that the gods might take it into their heads to divide man

into three parts, for the sake of still better fun. For the sake of still better fun; for is it not true, as I said, that love renders a person ridiculous, if not in the eyes of others certainly in the eyes of the gods?

Now, let me assume that the erotic element resides essentially in the relation between man and woman what is to be inferred from that? If the lover should say to his Lalage: I love you because you are a woman; I might as well love any other woman, as for instance, ugly Zoe: then beautiful Lalage would feel insulted.

In what, then, consists the lovable? This is my question; but unfortunately, no one has been able to tell me, The individual lover always believes that, as far as he is concerned, he knows. Still he cannot make himself understood by any other lover; and he who listens to the speech of a number of lovers will learn that no two of them ever agree, even though they all talk about the same thing. Disregarding those altogether silly explanations which leave one as wise as before, that is, end by asserting that it is really the pretty feet of the beloved damsel, or the admired mustachios of the swain, which are the objects of love disregarding these, one will find mentioned, even in the declamations of lovers in the higher style, first a number of details and, finally, the declaration: all her lovable ways; and when they have reached the climax: that inexplicable something I do not know how to explain. And this speech is meant to please especially beautiful Lalage. Me it does not please, for I don't understand a word of it and find, rather, that it contains a double contradiction first, that it ends with the inexplicable, second, that it ends with the inexplicable; for he who intends to end with the inexplicable had best begin with the inexplicable and then say no more, lest he lay himself open to suspicion. If he begin with the inexplicable, saying no more, then this does not prove his helplessness,

---

[1] Ibid., ch. 15-16.

for it is, anyway, an explanation in a negative sense; but if he does begin with something else and lands in the inexplicable, then this does certainly prove his helplessness.

So then we see: to love corresponds to the lovable; and the lovable is the inexplicable. Well, that is at least something; but comprehensible it is not, as little as the inexplicable way in which love seizes on its prey. Who, indeed, would not be alarmed if people about one, time and again, dropped down dead, all of a sudden, or had convulsions, without anyone being able to account for it? But precisely in this fashion does love invade life, only with the difference that one is not alarmed thereby, since the lovers themselves regard it as their greatest happiness, but that one, on the contrary, is tempted to laugh; for the comical and the tragical elements ever correspond to one another. Today, one may converse with a person and can fairly well make him out tomorrow, he speaks in tongues and with strange gestures: he is in love.

Now, if to love meant to fall in love with the first person that came along, it would be easy to understand that one could give no special reasons for it; but since to love means to fall in love with one, one single person in all the world, it would seem as if such an extraordinary process of singling out ought to be due to such an extensive chain of reasoning that one might have to beg to be excused from hear-ing it--not so much because it did not explain anything as because it might be too lengthy to listen to. But no, the lovers are not able to explain anything at all. He has seen hundreds upon hundreds of women; he is, perhaps, advanced in years and has all along felt nothing--and all at once he sees her, her the Only one, Catherine. Is this not comical? Is it not comical that the relation which is to explain and beautify all life, love, is not like the mustard seed from which there grows a great tree,[1] but being still smaller is, at bottom, nothing at all; for not a single antecedent criterion can be mentioned, as e.g., that the phenomenon occurred at a certain age, nor a single reason as to why be should select her, her alone in all the world and that by no means in the same sense as when "Adam chose Eve, because there was none other."[2]

Or is not the explanation which the lovers vouchsafe just as comical; or, does it not, rather, emphasize the comical aspect of love? They

---

[1] Cf. Matthew 13, 31, etc.
[2] A quotation from Musaeus, Volksmarchen der Deutschen, III,219.

say that love renders one blind, and by this fact they undertake to explain the phenomenon. Now, if a Person who was going into a dark room to fetch something should answer, on my advising him to take a light along, that it was only a trifling matter he wanted and so he would not bother to take a light along ah! then I would understand him excellently well. If, on the other hand, this same person should take me aside and, with an air of mystery, confide to me that the thing be was about to fetch was of the very greatest importance and that it was for this reason that he was able to do it in the dark ah! then I wonder if my weak mortal brain could follow the soaring flight of his speech. Even if I should refrain from laughing, in order not to offend him, I should hardly be able to restrain my mirth as soon as he had turned his back. But at love nobody laughs; for I am quite prepared to be embarrassed like the Jew who, after ending his story, asks: Is there no one who will laugh?[1] And yet I did not miss the point, as did the Jew, and as to my laughter I am far from wanting to insult any one. Quite on the contrary, I scorn those fools who imagine that their love has such good reasons that they can afford to laugh at other lovers; for since love is altogether inexplicable, one lover is as ridiculous as the other. Quite as foolish and haughty I consider it also when a man proudly looks about him in the circle of girls to find who may be worthy of him, or when a girl proudly tosses her head to select or reject; because such persons are simply basing their thoughts on an unexplained assumption. No. What busies my thought is love as such, and it is love which seems ridiculous to me; and therefore I fear it, lest I become ridiculous in my own eyes, or ridiculous in the eyes of the gods who have fashioned man thus. In other words, if love is ridiculous it is equally ridiculous, whether now my sweetheart be a princess or a servant girl; for the lovable, as we have seen, is the inexplicable.

Look you, therefore do I fear love, and find precisely in this a new proof of love's being comical; for my fear is so seriously tragic that it throws light on the comical nature love. When people wreck a building a sign is hung up to warn people, and I shall take care to stand from under; when a bar has been freshly painted a stone is laid in the road to apprise people of the fact; when a driver is in danger of running a man over he will shout "look out"; when there have been cases of cholera in a house a soldier is set as guard; and so forth. What I mean is that if

---

[1] The reference is to a situation in Richard Cumberland's (1732-1811) play of "The Jew," known to Copenhagen playgoers in an adaptation.

there is some danger, one may be warned and will successfully escape it by heeding the warning. Now, fearing to be rendered ridiculous by love, I certainly regard it as dangerous; so what shall I do to escape it? In other words, what shall I do to escape the danger of some woman falling in love with me? I am far from entertaining the thought of being an Adonis every girl is bound to fall in love with (relata refero,[1] for what this means I do not understand) -goodness no! But since I do not know what the lovable is I cannot, by any manners of means, know how to escape this danger. Since, for that matter, the very opposite of beauty may constitute the lovable; and, finally, since the inexplicable also is the lovable, I am forsooth in the same situation as the man Jean Paul speaks of somewhere who, standing on one foot, reads a sign saying, "fox-traps here," and now does not dare, either to lift his foot or to set it down. No, love any one I will not, before I have fathomed what love is; but this I cannot, but have, rather, come to the conclusion that it is comical. Hence I will not love-but alas! I have not thereby avoided the danger, for, since I do not know what the lovable is and how it seizes me, or how it seizes a woman with reference to me, I cannot make sure whether I have avoided the danger. This is tragical and, in a certain sense, even profoundly tragical, even if no one is concerned about it, or if no one is concerned about the bitter contradiction for one who thinks-that a something exists which everywhere exercises its power and yet is not to be definitely conceived by thought and which, perhaps, may attack from the rear him who in vain seeks to conceive it. But as to the tragic side of the matter it has its deep reason in the comic aspects just pointed out. Possibly, every other person will turn all this upside down and not find that to be comical which I do, but rather that which I conceive to be tragical; but this too proves that I am right to a certain extent. And that for which, if so happens, I become either a tragic or comic victim is plain enough, viz., my desire to reflect about all I do, and not imagine I am reflecting about life by dismissing its every important circumstance with an "I don't care, either way."

Man has both a soul and a body. About this the wisest and best of the race are agreed. Now, in case one assumes the essence of love to lie in the relation between man and woman, the comic aspect will show again in the face-about which is seen when the highest spiritual values express themselves in the most sensual terms. I am now refer-

---

[1] I relate what I have been told.

ring to all those extraordinary and mystic signals of love in short, to all the free-masonry which forms a continuation of the above-mentioned inexplicable something. The contradiction in which love here involves a person lies in the fact that the symbolic signs mean nothing at all or which amounts to the same that no one is able to explain what they do signify. Two loving souls vow that they will love each the other in all eternity; thereupon they embrace, and with a kiss they seal this eternal pact. Now I ask any thinking person whether he would have hit upon that! And thus there is constant shifting from the one to the other extreme in love. The most spiritual is expressed by its very opposite, and the sensual is to signify the most spiritual. Let me assume I am in love. In that case I would conceive it to be of the utmost importance to me that the one I love belonged to me for all time. This I comprehend; for I am now, really, speaking only of Greek eroticism which has to do with loving beautiful souls. Now when the person I love had vowed to return my love I would believe her or, in as far as there remained any doubt in me, try to combat my doubt. But what happens actually? For if I were in love I would, probably, behave like all the others, that is, seek to obtain still some other assurance than merely to believe her I love; which, though, is plainly the only assurance to *had.

When Cockatoo[1] all at once begins to plume himself like a duck which is gorged with food, and then emits the word "Marian," everybody will laugh, and so will I.. I suppose the spectator finds it comical that Cockatoo, who doesn't love Marian at all, should be on such intimate terms with her. But suppose, now, that Cockatoo does love Marian. Would that be comical still? To me it would; and the comical would seem to me to lie in love's having become capable of being expressed in such fashion. Whether now this has been the custom since the beginning of the world makes no difference whatsoever, for the comical has the prescriptive right from all eternity to be present in contradictions and here is a contradiction. There is really nothing comical in the antics of a manikin since we see someone pulling the strings. But to be a manikin at the beck of something inexplicable is indeed comical, for the contradiction lies in our not seeing any sensible reason why one should have to twitch now this leg and now that. Hence, if I cannot explain what I am doing, I do not care to do it; and if I cannot understand the power into whose sphere I am venturing, I

---

[1] A character in the Danish playwright Overskou's vaudeville of "Capriciosa" (Comedies III, 184).

do not care to surrender myself to that power. And if love is so mysterious a law which binds together the extremest contradictions, then who will guarantee that I might not, one day, become altogether confused? Still, that does not concern me so much.

Again, I have heard that some lovers consider the behavior of other lovers ridiculous. I cannot conceive how this ridicule is justified, for if this law of love be a natural law, then all lovers are subject to it; but if it be the law of their own choice, then those laughing lovers ought to be able to explain all about love; which, however, they are unable to do. But in this respect I understand this matter better as it seems a convention for one lover to laugh at the other because he always finds the other lover ridiculous, but not himself. If it be ridiculous to kiss an ugly girl, it is also ridiculous to kiss a pretty one; and the notion that doing this in some particular way should entitle one to cast ridicule on another who does it differently, is but presumptuousness and a conspiracy which does not, for all that, exempt such a snob from laying himself open to the ridicule which invariably results from the fact that no one is able to explain what this act of kissing signifies, whereas it is to signify all to signify, indeed, that the lovers desire to belong to each other in all eternity; aye, what is still more amusing, to render them certain that they will. Now, if a man should suddenly lay his head on one side, or shake it, or kick out with his leg and, upon my asking him why he did this, should answer "To be sure I don't know, myself, I just happened to do so, next time I may do something different, for I did it unconsciously" ah, then I would understand him quite well. But if he said, as the lovers say about their antics, that all bliss lay therein, how could I help finding it ridiculous just as I thought that other man's motions ridiculous, to be sure in a different sense until he restrained my laughter by declaring that they did not signify anything. For by doing so he removed the contradiction which is the basic cause of the comical. It is not at all comical that the insignificant is declared to signify nothing, but it is very much so if it be asserted to signify all.

As regards involuntary actions, the contradiction arises at the very outset because involuntary actions are not looked for in a free rational being. Thus if one supposed that the Pope had a coughing spell the very moment he was to place the crown on Napoleon's head; or that bride and groom, in the most solemn moment of the wedding ceremony should fall to sneezing-these would be examples of the comical, That is, the more a given action accentuates the free rational being, the more comical are involuntary actions. This holds true also in respect of the erotic gesticulations, where the comical element appears a second time, owing to the circumstance that the lovers attempt to explain away the contradiction by attributing to their gesticulations an absolute value. As is well known, children have a keen sense of the ridiculous witness children's testimony which can always be relied on in this regard. Now as a rule children , will laugh at lovers, and if one makes them tell what they have seen, surely no one can help laughing. This is, perhaps, due to the fact that children omit the point. Very strange! When the Jew omitted the point no one cared to laugh. Here, on the contrary, every one laughs because the point is omitted; since, however, no one can explain what the point is why, then there is no point at all.

So the lovers explain nothing; and those who praise love explain nothing but are merely intent on as one is bidden in the Royal Laws of Denmark on saying anent it all which may be pleasant and of good report. But a man who thinks, desires to have his logical categories in good order; and he who thinks about love wishes to be sure about his categories also in this matter. The fact is, though, that people do not think about love, and a "pastoral science" is still lacking; for even if a poet in a pastoral poem makes an attempt to show how love is born, everything is smuggled in again by help of another person who teaches the lovers how to love!

As we saw, the comical element in love arose from the face-about whereby the highest quality of one sphere does not find expression in that sphere but in the exactly opposite quality of another sphere. It is comical that the soaring flight of love-the desire to belong to each other for all time lands ever, like Saft,[1] in the pantry; but still more comical is it that this conclusion is said to constitute love's highest expression.

Wherever there is a contradiction, there the comical element is present also. I am ever following that track. If it be disconcerting to you, dear fellow banqueters, to follow me in what I shall have to say now, then follow me with averted countenances. I myself am speaking as if with veiled eyes; for as I see only the mystery in these matters, why, I cannot see, or I see nothing.

What is a consequence? If it cannot, in some way or other, be brought under the same head as its antecedent why, then it would be ridiculous if it posed as a consequence. To illustrate: if a man who wanted to take a bath jumped into the tank and, coming to the surface

---

[1] The glutton in Oehlenschloeger's vaudeville of "Sovedrikken."

again somewhat confused, groped for the rope to hold on to, but caught the douche-line by mistake, and a shower now descended on him with sufficient motivation and for excellent good reason why, then the consequence would be entirely in order. The ridiculous here consisted in his seizing the wrong rope; but there is nothing ridiculous in the shower descending when one pulls the proper rope. Rather, it would be ridiculous if it did not come; as for example, just to show the correctness of my contention about contradictions, if a man nerved himself with bold resolution in order to withstand the shock and, in the enthusiasm of his decision, with a stout heart pulled the line-and the shower did not come.

Let us see now how it is with regard to love. The lovers wish to belong to each other for all time, and this they express, curiously, by embracing each other with all the intensity of the moment; and all the bliss of love is said to reside therein. But all desire is egotistic. Now, to be sure, the lover's desire is not egotistic in respect of the one he loves, but the desire of both in conjunction is absolutely egotistic in so far as they in their union and love represent a new ego. And yet they are deceived; for in the same moment the race triumphs over the individual, the race is victorious, and the individuals are debased to do its bidding.

Now this I find more ridiculous than what Aristophanes thought so ridiculous. The ridiculous aspect of his theory of bi-section lies in the inherent contradiction (which the ancient author does not sufficiently emphasize, however). In considering a person one naturally supposes him to be an entity, and so one does believe till it becomes apparent that, under the obsession of love, he is but a half which runs about looking for its complement. There is nothing ridiculous in half an apple. The comical would appear if a whole apple turned out to be only half an apple. In the first case there exists no contradiction, but certainly in the latter. If one actually based one's reasoning on the figure of speech that woman is but half a person she would not be ridiculous at all in her love. Man, however, who has been enjoying civic rights as a whole person, will certainly appear ridiculous when he takes to running about (and looking for his other half);[1] for he betrays thereby that he is but half a person. In fact, the more one thinks about the matter the more ridiculous it seems; because if man really be a whole, why, then he will not become a whole in love, but he and woman would

---

[1] Supplied by the translator to complete the sense.

make up one and a half. No wonder, then, that the gods laugh, and particularly at man.

But let me return to my consequence. When the lovers have found each other, one should certainly believe that they formed a whole, and in this should lie the proof of their assertion that they wished to live for each other for all time. But lo! instead of living for each other they begin to live for the race, and this they do not even suspect.

What is a consequence? If, as I observed, one cannot detect in it the cause out of which it proceeded, the consequence is merely ridiculous, and he becomes a laughing stock to whom this happens. Now, the fact that the separated halves have found each other ought to be a complete satisfaction and rest for them; and yet the consequence is a new existence. That having found each other should mean a new existence for the lovers, is comprehensible enough; but not, that a new existence for a third being should take its inception from this fact. And yet the resulting consequence is greater than that of which it is the consequence, whereas such an end as the lovers' finding each other ought to be infallible evidence of no other, subsequent, consequence being thinkable.

Does the satisfaction of any other desire show an analogy to this consequence? Quite on the contrary, the satisfaction of desire is in every other case evinced by a period of rest; and even if a tristitia[1] does supervene indicating by the way, that every satisfaction of an appetite is comical this tristitia is a straightforward consequence, though no tristitia so eloquently attests a preceding comical element as does that following love. It is quite another matter with an enormous consequence such as we are dealing with, a consequence of which no one knows whence it comes, nor whether it will come; whereas, if it does come, it comes as a consequence.

Who is able to grasp this? And yet that which for the initiates of love constitutes the greatest pleasure is also the most important thing for them so important that they even adopt new names, derived from the consequence thereof which thus, curiously enough, assumes retroactive force, The lover is now called father, his sweetheart, mother; and these names seem to them the most beautiful. And yet there is a being to whom these names are even more beautiful; for what is as beautiful as filial piety? To me it seems the most beautiful of all sentiments; and fortunately I can appreciate the thought underlying it. We

---

[1] Dejection. Cf. the Maxim: omne animal post coitune [?] [Transcript unreadable] triste.

are taught that it is seeming in a son to love his father. This I comprehend, I cannot even suspect that there is any contradiction possible here, and I acknowledge infinite satisfaction in being held by the loving bonds of filial piety. I believe it is the greatest debt of all to owe another being one's life. I believe that this debt cannot ever be wiped out, or even fathomed by any calculation, and for this reason I agree with Cicero when he asserts that the son is always in the wrong as against his father; and it is precisely filial piety which teaches me to believe this, teaches me not even to penetrate the hidden, but rather to remain hidden in the father. Quite true, I am glad to be another person's greatest debtor; but as to the opposite, viz., before deciding to make another person my greatest debtor, I want to arrive at greater clarity. For to my conception there is a world of difference between being some person's debtor, and making some person one's debtor to such an extent that he will never be able to clear himself.

What filial piety forbids the son to consider, love bids the father to consider. And here contradiction sets in again. If the son has an immortal soul like his father, what does it mean, then, to be a father? For must I not smile at myself when thinking of myself as a father whereas the son is most deeply moved when he reflects on the relation he bears to his father? Very well do I understand Plato when he says that an animal will give birth to an animal of the same species, a plant, to a plant of the same species, and thus also man to man .[1] But this explains nothing, does not satisfy one's thought, and arouses but a dim feeling; for an immortal soul cannot be born. Whenever, then, a father considers his son in the light of his son's immortality which is, indeed, the essential consideration[2] he will probably smile at himself, for he cannot, by any means, grasp in their entirety all the beautiful and noble thoughts which his son with filial piety entertains about him. If, on the other hand, he considers his son from the point of view of his animal nature he must smile again, because the conception of fatherhood is too exalted an expression for it.

Finally, if it were thinkable that a father influenced his son in such fashion that his own nature was a condition from which the son's nature could not free itself, then the contradiction would arise in another direction; for in this case nothing more terrible is thinkable than being a father. There is no comparison between killing a person and giving

---

[1] This statement is to be found, rather, in Aristotle's Ethics II, 6.
[2] There is a pun here in the original.

him life the former decides his fate only in time, the other for all eternity. So there is a contradiction again, and one both to laugh and to weep about. Is paternity then an illusion even if not in the same sense as is implied in Magdelone's speech to Jeronymus[1] or is it the most terrible thought imaginable? Is it the greatest benefit conferred on one, or is it the sweetest gratification of one's desire is it something which just happens, or is it the greatest task of life ?

Look you, for this reason have I forsworn all love, for my thought is to me the most essential consideration. So even if love be the most exquisite joy, I renounce it, without wishing either to offend or to envy any one; and even if love be the condition for conferring the greatest benefit imaginable I deny myself the opportunity therefore but my thought I have not prostituted. By no means do I lack an eye for what is beautiful, by no means does my heart remain unmoved when I read the songs of the poets, by no means is my soul without sadness when it yields to the beautiful conception of love; but I do not wish to become unfaithful to my thought. And of what avail were it to be, for there is no happiness possible for me except my thought have free sway. If it had not, I would in desperation yearn for my thought, which I may not desert to cleave to a wife, for it is my immortal part and, hence, of more importance than a wife. Well do I comprehend that if anything is sacred it is love; that if faithlessness in any relation is base, it is doubly so in love; that if any deceit is detestable, it is tenfold more detestable in love. But my soul is innocent of blame. I have never looked at any woman to desire her, neither have I fluttered about aimlessly before blindly plunging, or lapsing, into the most decisive of all relations. If I knew what the lovable were I would know with certainty whether I had offended by tempting any one; but since I do not know, I am certain only of never having had the conscious desire to do so.

Supposing I should yield to love and be made to laugh; or supposing I should be cast down by terror, since I cannot find the narrow path which lovers travel as easily as if it were the broad highway, undisturbed by any doubts, which they surely have bestowed thought on (seeing our times have, indeed, reflected about all[2] and consequently will comprehend me when I assert that to act unreflectingly is nonsense, as one ought to have gone through all possible reflections before acting)supposing, I say, I should yield to love! Would I not in-

---

[1] In Holberg's comedy of "Erasmus Montanus," III,6.
[2] Cf. note p. 60.

sult past redress my beloved one if I laughed; or irrevocably plunge her into despair if I were overwhelmed by terror? For I understand well enough that a woman cannot be expected to have thought as profoundly about these matters; and a woman who found love comical (as but gods and men can, for which reason woman is a temptation luring them to become ridiculous) would both betray a suspicious amount of previous experience and understand me least. But a woman who comprehended the terror of love would have lost her loveliness and still fail to understand me she would be annihilated; which is in nowise my case, so long as my thought saves me.

Is there no one ready to laugh? When I began by wanting to speak about the comical element in love you perhaps, expected to be made to laugh, for it is easy to make you laugh, and I myself am a friend of laughter; and still you did not laugh, I believe. The effect of my speech was a different one, and yet precisely this proves that I have spoken about the comical. If there be no one who laughs at my speech well, then laugh a little at me, dear fellow-banqueters, and I shall not wonder; for I do not understand what I have occasionally heard you say about love. Very probably, though, you are among the initiated as I am not.

Thereupon the Young Person seated himself. He had become more beautiful, almost, than before the meal. Now, he sat quietly, looking down before him, unconcerned about the others. John the Seducer desired at once to urge some objections against the Young Person's speech but was interrupted by Constantin who warned against discussions and ruled that on this occasion only speeches were in order. John said if that was the case, he would stipulate that he should be allowed to be the last speaker. This again gave rise to a discussion as to the order in which they were to speak, which Constantin closed by offering to speak forth with, against their recognizing his authority to appoint the speakers in their turn.

(Constantin's Speech)

Constantin spoke as follows:
There is a time to keep silence, and a time to speak,[1] and now it seems to be the time to speak briefly, for our young friend has spoken

---

[1] Eccles. 3, 7.

much and very strangely. His vis comica[1] has made us struggle ancipiti proelio[2] because his speech was full of doubts, as he himself is, sitting there now a perplexed man who knows not whether to laugh, or weep, or fall in love. In fact, had I had foreknowledge of his speech, such as he demands one should have of love, I should have forbidden him to speak; but now it is too late. I shall bid you then, dear fellow-banqueters, "gladsome and merry to be," and even if I cannot enforce this I shall ask you to forget each speech so soon as it is made and to wash it down with a single draught.

And now as to woman, about whom I shall speak. I too have pondered about her, and I have finally discovered the category to which she belongs. I too have sought, but I have found, too, and I have made a matchless discovery which I shall now communicate to you. Woman is understood correctly only when placed in the category of "the joke."

It is man's function to be absolute, to act in an absolute fashion, or to give expression to the absolute. Woman's sphere lies in her relativity.[3] Between beings so radically different, no true reciprocal relation can exist. Precisely in this incommensurability lies the joke. And with woman the joke was born into the world. It is to be understood, however, that man must know how to stick to his role of being absolute; for else nothing is seen that is to say, something exceedingly common is seen, viz., that man and woman fit each other, he as a half man and she as a half man.

The joke is not an æsthetic, but an abortive ethical, category. Its effect on thought is about the same as the impression we receive if a man were solemnly to begin making a speech, recite a comma or two with his pronouncement, then say "hm!"–dash"–and then stop. Thus with woman. One tries to cover her with the ethical category, one thinks of human nature, one opens one's eyes, one fastens one's glances on the most excellent maiden in question, an effort is made to redeem the claims of the ethical demand; and then one grows ill at ease and says to one's self: ah, this is undoubtedly a joke! The joke lies, indeed, in applying that category to her and measuring her by it, because it would be idle to expect serious results from her; but just that

---

[1] Comical power.
[2] In uncertain battle.
[3] According to the development of these terms in Kierkegaard's previous works, the "absolute" belongs to the ethic, the "relative" to the æsthetic sphere.

is the joke. Because if one could demand it of her it would not be a joke at all. A mighty poor joke indeed it would be, to place her under the air-pump and draw the air out of her–indeed it were a shame; but to blow her up to supernatural size and let her imagine herself to have attained all the ideality which a little maiden of sixteen imagines she has, that is the beginning of the game and, indeed, the beginning of a highly entertaining performance. No youth has half so much imaginary ideality as a young girl, but: "We shall soon be even" as says the tailor in the proverb; for her ideality is but an illusion.

If one fails to consider woman from this point of view she may cause irreparable harm; but through my conception of her she becomes harmless and amusing. For a man there is nothing more shocking than to catch himself twaddling. It destroys all true ideality; for one may repent of having been a rascal, and one may feel sorry for not having meant a word of what one said; but to have talked nonsense, sheer nonsense, to have meant all one said and behold! it was all nonsense– that is too disgusting for repentance incarnate to put up with. But this is not the case with woman. She has a prescriptive right to transfigure herself-in less than 24 hours–in the most innocent and pardonable nonsense; for far is it from her ingenuous soul to wish to deceive one! indeed, she meant all she said, and now she says the precise opposite, but with the same amiable frankness, for now she is willing to stake everything on what she said last. Now in case a man in all seriousness surrenders to love he may be called fortunate indeed if he succeeds in obtaining an insurance–if, indeed, he is able to obtain it anywhere; for so inflammable a material as woman is most likely to arouse the suspicions of an insurance agent. Just consider for a moment what he has done in thus identifying himself with her! If, some fine New Year's night she goes off like some fireworks he will promptly follow suit; and even if this should not happen he will have many a close call. And what may he not lose! He may lose his all; for there is but one absolute antithesis to the absolute, and that is nonsense. Therefore, let him not seek refuge in some society for morally tainted individuals, for he is not morally tainted—far from it; only, he has been reduced in absurdum and beatified in nonsense; that is, has been made a fool of.

This will never happen among men. If a man should sputter off in this fashion I would scorn him. If he should fool me by his cleverness I need but apply the ethical category to him, and the danger is trifling. If things go too far I shall put a bullet through his brain; but to challenge a woman-what is that, if you please? Who does not see that it is a joke, just as when Xerxes had the sea whipped? When Othello murders Desdemona, granting she really had been guilty, he has gained nothing, for he has been duped, and a dupe he remains; for even by his murdering her he only makes a concession with regard to a consequence which originally made him ridiculous; whereas Elvira[1] may be an altogether pathetic figure when arming herself with a dagger to obtain revenge. The fact that Shakespeare has conceived Othello as a tragic figure (even disregarding the calamity that Desdemona is innocent) is to be explained and, indeed, to perfect satisfaction, by the hero being a colored person. For a colored person, dear fellow-banqueters, who cannot be assumed to represent spiritual qualities—a colored person, I say, who therefore becomes green in his face when his ire is aroused (which is a physiological fact), a colored man may, indeed, become tragic if he is deceived by a woman; just as a woman has all the pathos of tragedy on her side when she is betrayed by a man. A man who flies into a rage may perhaps become tragic; but a man of whom one may expect a developed mentality, he either not become jealous, or he will become ridiculous if does; and most of all when he comes running with a dagger in his hand.

A Pity that Shakespeare has not presented us with a comedy of this description in which the claim raised by a woman's infidelity is turned down by irony; for not everyone who is able to see the comical element in this situation is able also to develop the thought and give it dramatic embodiment. Let one but imagine Socrates surprising Xanthippe in the act—for it would be un-Socratic even to think of Socrates being particularly concerned about his wife's infidelity, or still worse, spying on her—imagine it, and I believe that the fine smile which transformed the ugliest man in Athens into the handsomest, would for the first time have turned into a roar of laughter. It is incomprehensible why Aristophanes, who so frequently made Socrates the butt of his ridicule, neglected to have him run on the stage shouting: "Where is she, where is she, so that I may kill her, i.e., my unfaithful Xanthippe." For really it does not matter greatly whether or no Socrates was made a cuckold, and all that Xanthippe may do in this regard is wasted labor, like snapping one's fingers in one's pocket; for Socrates remains the same intellectual hero, even with a horn on his forehead. But if he had in fact become jealous and had wanted to kill Xanthippe—alas! then would Xanthippe have exerted a power over

---

[1] Heroine of Mozart's "Don Juan."

him such as the entire Greek nation and his sentence of death could not—to make him ridiculous.

A cuckold is comical, then, with respect to his wife; but he may be regarded as becoming tragical with respect to other men. In this fact we may find an explanation of the Spanish conception of honor. But the tragic element resides chiefly in his not being able to obtain redress, and the anguish of his suffering consists really in its being devoid of meaning—which is terrible enough. To shoot the woman, to challenge her, to despise her, all this would only serve to render the poor man still more ridiculous; for woman is the weaker sex. This consideration enters in everywhere and confuses all. If she performs a great deed she is admired more than man, because it is more than was expected of her. If she is betrayed, all the pathos is on her side; but if a man is deceived one has scant sympathy and little patience while he is present—and laughs at him while his back is turned.

Look you, therefore is it advisable betimes to consider woman as a joke. The entertainment she affords is simply incomparable. Let one consider her a fixed quantity, and one's self a relative one; let one by no means contradict her, for that would simply be helping her; let one never doubt what she says but, rather, believe her every word; let one gallivant about her, with eyes rendered unsteady unspeakable admiration and blissful intoxication, and with the mincing steps of a worshipper; let one languishingly fall on one's knees, then lift up one's eyes up to her languishingly and heave a breath again; let one do all she bids one, like an obedient slave. And now comes the cream of the joke. We need no proof that woman can speak, i.e., use words. Unfortunately, however, she does not possess sufficient reflection for making sure against her in the long run—which is, at most, eight days—contradicting herself; unless indeed man, by contradicting her, exerts a regulative influence. So the consequence is that within a short time confusion will reign supreme. If one had not done what she told one to, the confusion would pass unnoticed; for she forgets again as quickly as she talks. But since her admirer has done all, and has been at her beck and call in every instance, the confusion is only too glaring.

The more gifted the woman, the more amusing the situation. For the more gifted she is, the more imagination she will possess. Now, the more imagination she possesses, the greater airs she will give herself and the greater the confusion which is bound to become evident in the next instant. In life, such entertainment is rarely had, because this blind obedience to a woman's whims occurs but seldom. And if it does, in some languishing swain, most likely he is not qualified to see the fun. The fact is, the ideality a little maiden assumes in moments when her imagination is at work is encountered nowhere else, whether in gods or man; but it is all the more entertaining to believe her and to add fuel to the fire.

As I remarked, the fun is simply incomparable—indeed, I know it for a fact, because I have at times not been able to sleep at night with the mere thought of what new confusions I should live to see, through the agency of my sweetheart and my humble zeal to please her. Indeed, no one who gambles in a lottery will meet with more remarkable combinations than he who has a passion for this game. For this is sure, that every woman without exception possesses the same qualifications for being resolved and transfigured in nonsense with a gracefulness, a nonchalance, an assurance such as befits the weaker sex.

Being a right-minded lover one naturally discovers every possible charm in one's beloved. Now, when discovering genius in the above sense, one ought not to let it remain a mere possibility but ought, rather, to develop it into virtuosity. I do not need to be more specific, and more cannot be said in a general way, yet everyone will understand me. Just as one may find entertainment in balancing a cane on one's nose, in swinging a tumbler in a circle without spilling a drop, in dancing between eggs, and in other games as amusing and profitable, likewise, and not otherwise, in living with his beloved the lover will have a source of incomparable entertainment and food for most interesting study. In matters pertaining to love let one have absolute belief, not only in her protestations of fidelity—one soon tires of that game—but in all those explosions of inviolable Romanticism by which she would probably perish if one did not contrive a safety-valve through which the sighs and the smoke, and "the aria of Romanticism[1]" may escape and make her worshipper happy. Let one compare her admiringly to Juliet, the difference being only that no person ever as much as thought of touching a hair on her Romeo's head. With regard to intellectual matters, let one hold her capable of all and, if one has been lucky enough to find the right woman, in a trice one will have a cantankerous authoress, whilst wonderingly shading one's eyes with one's hand and duly admiring what the little black hen may yield besides.[2] It

---

[1] Quotations from Wessel's famous comedy of "Love without Stockings," III, 3.
[2] Viz. besides the eggs she duly furnishes; Holberg, "The Busybody," II, 1.

is altogether incomprehensible why Socrates did not choose this course of action instead of bickering with Xanthippe—oh, well! to be sure he wished to acquire practice, like the riding master who, even though he has the best trained horse, yet knows how to tease him in such fashion that there is good reason for breaking him in again."[1]

Let me be a little more concrete, in order to illustrate a particular and highly interesting phenomenon. A great deal has been said about feminine fidelity, but rarely with any discretion.[2] From a purely æsthetic point of view this fidelity is to be regarded as a piece of poetic fiction which steps on the stage to find her lover—a fiction which sits by the spinning wheel and waits for her lover to come; but when she has found him, or he has come, why, then æsthetics is at a loss. Her infidelity, on the other hand, as contrasted with her previous fidelity, is to be judged chiefly with regard to its ethical import, when jealousy will appear as a tragic passion. There are three possibilities, so the case is favorable for woman; for there are two cases of fidelity, as against one of infidelity. Inconceivably great is her fidelity when she is not altogether sure of her cavalier; and ever so inconceivably great is it when he repels her fidelity. The third case would be her infidelity. Now granted one has sufficient intellect and objectivity to make reflections, one will find sufficient justification, in what has been said, for my category of "the joke." Our young friend whose beginning in a manner deceived me seemed to be on the point of entering into this matter, but backed out again, dismayed at the difficulty. And yet the explanation is not difficult, providing one really sets about it seriously, to make unrequited love and death correspond to one another, and providing one is serious enough to stick to his thought—and so much seriousness one ought to have—for sake of the joke.

Of course this phrase of unrequited love being death originated either with a woman or a womanish male. Its origin is easily made out, seeing that it is one of those categorical outbursts which, spoken with great bravado, on the spur of the moment, may count on a great and immediate applause; for although this business is said to be a matter of life and death, yet the phrase is meant for immediate consumption—like cream-puffs. Although referring to daily experience it by no

---

[1] This figure is said by Diogenes Laertios II,37 to have been used by Socrates himself about his relation to Xanthippe.
[2] The following sentences are not as clear in meaning as is otherwise the case in Kierkegaard.

means binding on him who is to die, but only obliges the listener to rush post-haste to the assistance of the dying lover. If a man should take to using such phrases it would not be amusing at all, for he would be too despicable to laugh at. Woman, however, possesses genius, is lovable in the measure she possesses it, and is amusing at all times. Well, then, the languishing lady dies of love—why certainly, for did she not say so herself? In this matter she is pathetic, for woman has enough courage to say what no man would have the courage to do—so then she dies! In saying so I have measured her by ethical standards. Do ye likewise, dear fellow-banqueters, and understand your Aristotle aright, now! He observes very correctly that woman cannot be used in tragedy.[1] And very certainly, her proper sphere is the pathetic and serious divertissement, the half-hour face, not the five-act drama. So then she dies. But should she for that reason not be able to love again? Why not?—that is, if it be possible to restore her to life. Now, having been restored to life, she is of course a new being—another person, that is, and begins afresh and falls in love for the first time: nothing remarkable in that! Ah, death, great is thy power; not the most violent emetic and not the most powerful laxative could ever have the same purging effect!

The resulting confusion is capital, if one but is attentive and does not forget. A dead man is one of the most amusing characters to be met with in life. Strange that more use is not made of him on the stage, for in life he is seen, now and then. When you come to think of it, even one who has only been seemingly dead is a comical figure; but one who was really dead certainly contributes to our entertainment all one can reasonably expect of a man. All depends on whether one is attentive. I myself had my attention called to it, one day, as I was walking with one of my acquaintances. A couple passed us. I judged from the expression on his face that he knew them and asked whether that was the case. "Why, yes," he answered, "I know them very well, and especially the lady, for she is my departed one."—"What departed one?" I asked.—"Why, my departed first love," he answered. "Indeed, this is a strange affair. She said: I shall die. And that very same moment she departed, naturally enough, by death—else one might have insured her beforehand in the widow's insurance. Too late! Dead she was and dead she remained; and now I wander about, as says the poet, vainly seeking the grave of my lady-love that I may shed my tears thereon." Thus

---

[1] Poetics, chap.15.

this broken-hearted man who remained alone in the world, though it consoled him to find her pretty far along with some other man.

It is a good thing for the girls, thought I, that they don't have to be buried, every time they die; for if parents have hitherto considered a boy-child to be the more expensive, the girls might become even more so!

A simple ease of infidelity is not as amusing, by far. I mean, if a girl should fall in love with someone else and should say to her lover: "I cannot help it, save me from myself!" But to die from sorrow because she cannot endure being separated from her lover by his journey to the West Indies, to have put up with his departure, however, and then, at his return, be not only not dead, but attached to someone else for all time—that certainly is a strange fate for a lover to undergo. No wonder, then, that the heart-broken man at times consoled himself with the burthen of an old song which runs: "Hurrah for you and me, I say, we never shall forget that day!"

Now forgive me, dear fellow-banqueters, if I have spoken at too great length; and empty a glass to love and to woman. Beautiful she is and lovely, if she be considered æsthetically. That is undeniable. But, as has often been said, and as I shall say also: one ought not to remain standing here, but should go on.[1] Consider her, then, ethically and you will hardly have begun to do so before the humor of it will become apparent. Even Plato and Aristotle assume that woman is an imperfect form, an irrational quantity, that is, one which might some time, in a better world, be transformed into a man. In this life one must take her as she is. And what this is becomes apparent very soon; for she will not be content with the æsthetic sphere, but goes on, she wants to become emancipated, and she has the courage to say so. Let her wish be fulfilled and the amusement will be simply incomparable.

When Constantin had finished speaking he forthwith ruled Victor Eremita to begin. He spoke as follows:

(Victor Eremita's Speech)

As will be remembered, Plato offers thanks to the gods for four things. In the fourth place he is grateful for having been permitted to

---

[1] Cf. note p. 60. [re: footnote 11 of this document.]

be a contemporary of Socrates. For the three other boons mentioned by him,[1] an earlier Greek philosopher[2] had already thanked the gods, and so I conclude that they are worthy our gratitude. But alas!—even if I wanted to express my gratitude like these Greeks I would not be able to do so for what was denied me. Let me then collect my soul in gratitude for the one good which was conferred on me also—that I was made a man and not a woman.

To be a woman is something so curious, so heterogeneous and composite that no predicate will fully express these qualities; and if I should use many predicates they would contradict one another in such fashion that only a woman would be able to tolerate the result and, what is worse, feel happy about it. The fact that she really signifies less than man—that is not her misfortune, and still less so if she got to know it, for it might be borne with fortitude. No, her misfortune consists in her life's having become devoid of fixed meaning through a romantic conception of things, by virtue of which, now she signifies all, and now, nothing at all; without ever finding out what she really does signify and even that is not her misfortune but, rather, the fact that, being a woman, she never will be able to find out. As for myself, if I were a woman, I should prefer to be one in the Orient and as a slave; for to be a slave, neither more nor less is at any rate something, in comparison with being, now heyday, now nothing.

Even if a woman's life did not contain such contrasts, the distinction she enjoys, and which is rightly assumed to be hers as a woman—a distinction she does not share with man—would by itself point to the meaninglessness of her life. The distinction I refer to is that of gallantry. To be gallant to woman is becoming in men. Now gallantry consists very simply in conceiving in fantastic categories that person to whom one is gallant. To be gallant to a man is, therefore, an insult, for he begs to be excused from the application of fantastic categories to him. For the fair sex, however, gallantry signifies a tribute, a distinction, which is essentially its privilege. Ah me, if only a single cavalier were gallant to them the case would not be so serious. But far from it! At bottom every man is gallant, he is unconsciously so. This signifies, therefore, that it is life itself which has bestowed this perquisite on the fair sex. Woman on her part unconsciously accepts it. Here

---

[1] They are, that he had been created a man and not an animal, a man and not a woman, a Greek and not a Barbarian (Lactantius, Instit.)III, 19,17).
[2] Thales of Miletos (Diogenes Laertios I, 33).

we have the same trouble again; for if only a single woman did so, another explanation would be necessary. This is life's characteristic irony.

Now if gallantry contained the truth it ought to be reciprocal, i.e., gallantry would be the accepted quotation for the stated difference between beauty on the one hand, and power, astuteness, and strength, on the other. But this is not the case, gallantry is essentially woman's due; and the fact that she unconsciously accepts it may be explained through the solicitude of nature for the weak and those created in a stepmotherly fashion by her, who feel more than recompensed by an illusion. But precisely this illusion is misfortune. It is not seldom the case that nature comes to the assistance of an afflicted creature by consoling him with the notion that he is the most beautiful. If that is so, why, then we may say that nature made good the deficiency since now the creature is endowed with even more than could be reasonably demanded. But to be beautiful -only in one's imagination, and not to be overcome, indeed, by sadness, but to be fooled into an illusion—why, that is still worse mockery. Now, as to being afflicted, woman certainly is far from having been treated in a stepmotherly fashion by nature; still she is so in another sense inasmuch as she never can free herself from the illusion with which life has consoled her.

Gathering together one's impressions of a woman's existence, in order to point out its essential features, one is struck by the fact that every woman's life gives one an entirely phantastic impression. In a far more decisive sense than man she may be said to have turning points in her career; for her turning points turn everything upside down. In one of Tieck's[1] Romantic dramas there occurs a person who, having once been king of Mesopotamia, now is a green-grocer in Copenhagen. Exactly as fantastic is every feminine existence. If the girl's name is Juliana, her life is as follows: erstwhile empress in the wide domains of love, and titulary queen of all the exaggerations of tomfoolery; now, Mrs. Peterson, corner Bath Street.

When a child, a girl is less highly esteemed than a boy. When a little older, one does not know exactly what to make of her. At last she enters that decisive period in which she holds absolute sway. Worshipfully man approaches her as a suitor. Worshipfully, for so does every suitor, it is not the scheme of a crafty deceiver. Even the executioner, when laying down his fasces to go a-wooing, even he bends his knee,

---

[1] German poet of the Romantic School (1773-1853).

although he is willing to offer himself up, within a short time, to domestic executions which he finds so natural that he is far from seeking any excuse for them in the fact that public executions have grown so few. The cultured person behaves in the very same manner. He kneels, he worships, he conceives his lady-love in the most fantastic categories; and then he very quickly forgets his kneeling position—in fact, he knew full well the while he knelt that it was fantastic to do so.

If I were a woman I would prefer to be sold by my father to the highest bidder, as is the custom in the Orient; for there is at least some sense in such a deal. What misfortune to have been born a woman! Yet her misfortune really consists in her not being able to comprehend it, being a woman. If she does complain, she complains rather about her Oriental, than her Occidental, status. But if I were a woman I would first of all refuse to be wooed, and resign myself to belong to the weaker sex, if such is the case, and be careful—which is most important if one is proud—of not going beyond the truth. However, that is of but little concern to her. Juliana is in the seventh heaven, and Mrs. Peterson submits to her fate.

Let me, then, thank the gods that I was born a man and not a woman. And still, how much do I forego! For is not all poetry, from the drinking song to the tragedy, a deification of woman? All the worse for her and for him who admires her; for if he does not look out he will, all of a sudden, have to pull a long face. The beautiful, the excellent, all of man's achievement, owes its origin to woman, for she inspires him. Woman is, indeed, the inspiring element in life. How many a love-lorn shepherd has played on this theme, and how many a shepherdess has listened to it! Verily, my soul is without envy and feels only gratitude to the gods; for I would rather be a man, though in humble station, but really so, than be a woman and an indeterminate quantity, rendered happy by a delusion—I would rather be a concrete thing, with a small but definite meaning, than an abstraction which is to mean all.

As I have said, it is through woman that ideality is born into the world and—what were man without her! There is many a man who has become a genius through a woman, many a one a hero, many a one a poet, many a one even a saint; but he did not become a genius through the woman he married, for through her he only became a privy councillor; he did not become a hero through the woman he married, for through her he only became a general; he did not become a poet through the woman he married, for through her he only became a father; he did not become a saint through the woman he married, for he did not marry, and would have married but one—the one whom he did not marry; just as the others became a genius, became a hero, became a poet through the help of the woman they did not marry. If woman's ideality were in itself inspiring, why, then the inspiring woman would be the one to whom a man is united for life. But life tells a different story. It is only by a negative relation to her that man is rendered productive in his ideal endeavors. In this sense she is inspiring; but to say that she is inspiring, without qualifying one's statement, is to be guilty of a paralogism[1] which one must be a woman to overlook. Or has anyone ever heard of any man having become a poet through his wife? So long as man does not possess her she inspires him. It is this truth which gives rise to the illusions entertained in poetry and by women. The fact that he does not possess her signifies, either, that he is still fighting for her—thus has woman inspired many a one and rendered him a knight; but has anyone ever heard of any man having been rendered a knight valiant through his wife? Or, the fact that he does not possess her signifies that he cannot obtain her by any manner of means—thus has woman inspired many a one and roused his ideality; that is, if there is anything in him worthwhile. But a wife, who has things ever so much worthwhile for her husband, will hardly arouse any ideal strivings in him. Or, again, the fact that be does not possess her signifies that he is pursuing an ideal. Perchance he loves many, but loving many is also a kind of unrequited love; and yet the ideality of his soul is to be seen in this striving and yearning, and not in the small bits of lovableness which make up the sum total of the contributions of all those he loves.

The highest ideality a woman can arouse in a man consists, in fact, in the awakening within him of the consciousness of immortality. The point of this proof lies in what one might call the necessity of a reply. Just as one may remark about some play that it cannot end without this or that person getting in his say, likewise (says ideality) our existence cannot be all over with death: I demand a reply! This proof is frequently furnished, in a positive fashion, in the public advertiser. I hold that to be entirely proper, for if proof is to be made in the public advertiser it must be made in a positive fashion. Thus: Mrs. Petersen, we learn, has lived a number of years, until in the night of the 24th it pleased Providence, etc. This produces in Mr. Petersen an attack of reminiscences from his courting days or, to express it quite plainly, nothing

---

[1] Reasoning against the rules of logic.

but seeing her again will ever console him. For this blissful meeting he prepare himself, in the meanwhile, by taking unto himself another wife; for, to be sure, this marriage is by no means as poetic as the first—still it is a good imitation. This is the proof positive. Mr. Petersen is not satisfied with demanding a reply, no, he wants a meeting again in the hereafter.

As is well known, a base metal will often show the gleam of precious metal. This is the brief silver-gleam. With respect to the base metal this is a tragic moment, for it must once for all resign itself to being a base metal. Not so with Mr. Petersen. The possession of ideality is by rights inherent in every person—and now, if I laugh at Mr. Petersen it is not because he, being in reality of base metal, had but a single silver-gleam; but, rather, because just this silver-gleam betrays his having become a base metal. Thus does the philistine look most ridiculous when, arrayed in ideality, he affords fitting occasion to say, with Holberg: What! does that cow wear a fine dress, too?[1]

The case is this: whenever a woman arouses ideality in man, and thereby the consciousness of immortality, she always does so negatively. He who really became a genius, hero, a poet, a saint through woman, he has by that very fact seized on the essence of immortality. Now if the inspiring element were positively present in woman, why, then a man's wife, and only his wife, ought to awaken in the consciousness of immortality. But the reverse holds true. That is, if she is really to awaken ideality in husband she must die. Mr. Petersen, to be sure, is not affected, for all that. But if woman, by her death, does awaken man's ideality, then is she indeed the cause of all the great things poetry attributes to her; but note well: that which she did in a positive fashion for him in no wise roused his ideality. In fact, her significance in this regard becomes the more doubtful the longer she lives, because she will at length really begin to wish to signify something positive. However, the more positive the proof the less it proves; for then Mr. Petersen's longing will be for some past common experiences whose content was, to all intents and purposes, exhausted when they were had. Most positive of all the proof becomes if the object of his longing concerns their marital spooning—that time when they visited the Deer Park together! In the same way one might suddenly feel a longing for the old pair of slippers one used to be so comfortable in; but that proof is not exactly a proof for the immortality

---

[1] "The Lying-in Room," II, 2.

of the soul. On the other hand, the more negative the proof, the better it is; for the negative is higher than the positive, inasmuch as it concerns our immortality, and is thus the only positive value.

Woman's main significance lies in her negative contribution, whereas her positive contributions are as nothing in comparison but, on the contrary, pernicious. It is this truth which life keeps from her, consoling her with an illusion which surpasses all that might arise in any man's brain, and with parental care ordering life in such fashion that both language and everything else confirm her in her illusion. For even if she be conceived as the very opposite of inspiring, and rather as the well-spring of all corruption; whether now we imagine that with her, sin came into the world, or that it is her infidelity which ruined all—our conception of her is always gallant. That is, when hearing such opinions one might readily assume that woman were really able to become infinitely more culpable than man, which would, indeed, amount to an immense acknowledgment of her powers. Alas, alas! the case is entirely different. There is a secret reading of this text which woman cannot comprehend; for, the very next moment, all life owns to the same conception as the state, which makes man responsible for his wife. One condemns her as man never is condemned (for only a real sentence is passed on him, and there the matter ends), not with her receiving a milder sentence; for in that case not all of her life would be an illusion, but with the case against her being dismissed and the public, i.e., life, having to defray the costs. One moment, woman is supposed to be possessed of all possible wiles, the next moment, one laughs at him whom she deceived, which surely is a contradiction. Even such a case as that of Potiphar's wife does not preclude the possibility of her having really been seduced. Thus has woman an enormous possibility, such as no man has—an enormous possibility; but her reality is in proportion. And most terrible of all is the magic of illusion in which she feels herself happy.

Let Plato then thank the gods for having been born a contemporary of Socrates: I envy him; let him offer thanks for being a Greek: I envy him; but when he is grateful for having been born a man and not a woman I join him with all my heart. If I had been born a woman and could understand what now I can understand—it were terrible! But if I had been born a woman and therefore could not understand it—that were still more terrible!

But if the case is as I stated it, then it follows that one had better refrain from any positive relation with woman. Wherever she is concerned one has to reckon with that inevitable hiatus which renders her happy as she does not detect the illusion, but which would be a man's undoing if he detected it.

I thank the gods, then, that I was born a man and not a woman; and I thank them, furthermore, that no woman by some life-long attachment holds me in duty bound to be constantly reflecting that it ought not to have been.

Indeed, what a passing strange device is marriage! And what makes it all the stranger is the suggestion that it is to be a step taken without thought. And yet no step is more decisive, for nothing in life is as inexorable and masterful as the marriage tie. And now so important a step as marriage ought, so we are told, to be taken without reflection! Yet marriage is not something simple but something immensely complex and indeterminate. Just as the meat of the turtle smacks of all kinds of meat, so likewise does marriage have a taste of all manner of things; and just as the turtle is a sluggish animal, likewise is marriage a sluggish thing. Falling in love is, at least, a simple thing, but marriage—! Is it something heathen or something Christian, something spiritual or something profane, or something civil, or something of all things? Is it an expression of an inexplicable love, the elective affinity of souls in delicate accord with one another; or is it a duty, or a partnership, or a mere convenience, or the custom of certain countries or is it a duty, or a partnership, or a mere convenience, or the custom of certain countries—or is it a little of all these? Is one to order the music for it from the town musician or the organist, or is one to have a little from both? Is it the minister or the police sergeant who is to make the speech and enroll the names in the book of life—or in the town register? Does marriage blow a tune on a comb, or does it listen to the whisperings "like to those of the fairies from the grottoes of a summer night"[1]

And now every Darby imagines he performed such a Potpourri, such incomparably complex music, in getting married—and imagines that he is still performing it while living a married life! My dear fellow-banqueters, ought we not, in default of a wedding present and congratulations, give each of the conjugal partners a demerit for re-peated inattentiveness? It is taxing enough to express a single idea in one's life; but to think something so complicated as marriage and, consequently, bring it under one head; to think something so complicated and yet to do jus-tice to each and every element in it, and have

---

[1] A quotation from Oehlenschläger's "Aladdin."

everything present at the same time—verily, he is a great man who can accomplish all this! And still every Benedict accom-plishes it—so he does, no doubt; for does he not say that he does it unconsciously? But if this is to be done uncon-sciously it must be through some higher form of uncon-sciousness permeating all one's reflective powers. But not a word is said about this! And to ask any married man about it means just wasting one's time.

He who has once committed a piece of folly will con-stantly be pursued by its consequences. In the case of mar-riage the folly consists in one's having gotten into a mess, and the punishment, in recognizing, when it is too late, what one has done. So you will find that the married man, now, becomes chesty, with a bit of pathos, thinking he has done something remarkable in having entered wedlock; now, puts his tail between his legs in dejection; then again, praises marriage in sheer self-defense. But as to a thought-unit which might serve to hold together the disjecta membra[1] of the most heterogeneous conceptions of life contained in marriage—for that we shall wait in vain.

Therefore, to be a mere Benedict is humbug, and to be a seducer is humbug, and to wish to experiment with woman for the sake of "the joke" is also humbug. In fact, the two last mentioned methods will be seen to involve concessions to woman on the part of man quite as large as those found in marriage. The seducer wishes to rise in his own es-tima-tion by deceiving her; but this very fact that he deceives and wishes to deceive—that he cares to deceive, is also a demonstration of his dependence on woman. And the same is true of him who wishes to experiment with her.

If I were to imagine any possible relation with woman it would be one so saturated with reflection that it would, for that very reason, no longer be any relation with her at all. To be an excellent husband and yet on the sly seduce every girl; to seem a seducer and yet harbor with-in one all the ardor of romanticism—there would be something to that, or the concession in the first instance were then annihilated in the second. Certain it is that man finds his true ideality only in such a re-duplication. All merely unconscious ex-istence must be obliterated, and its obliteration ever cun-ningly guarded by some sham expression. Such a reduplication is incomprehensible to woman, for it removes from her the possibility of expressing man's true nature in one form. If it were possible for woman to exist in such a reduplication, no erotic

---

[1] Scattered members.

relation with her were thinkable. But, her nature being such as we all know it to be, any disturbance of the erotic relation is brought about by man's true nature which ever consists precisely in the annihilation of that in which she has her being.

Am I then preaching the monastic life and rightly called Eremita? By no means. You may as well eliminate the cloister, for after all it is only a direct expression of spirit-uality and as such but a vain endeavor to express it in direct terms. It makes small difference whether you use gold, or silver, or paper money; but he who does not spend a farthing but is counterfeit, he will comprehend me. He to whom every direct expression is but a fraud, he and he only, is safeguarded better than if he lived in a cloister-cell—he will be a hermit even if he travelled in an omnibus and night.

Scarcely had Victor finished when the Dressmaker jumped to his feet and threw over a bottle of wine standing before him; then he spoke as follows:

(The Dressmaker's Speech)

Well spoken, dear fellow-banqueters, well spoken! The longer I hear you speak the more I grow convinced that you are fellow-conspirators—I greet you as such, I understand you as such; for fellow-conspirators one can make out from afar. And yet, what know you? What does your bit of theory to which you wish to give the appearance of experience, your bit of experience which you make over into a theory—what does it amount to? For every now and then you believe her a moment and—are caught in a moment! No, I know woman—from her weak side, that is to say, I know her. I shrink from no means to make sure about what I have learned; for I am a madman, and a madman one must be to understand her, and if one has not been one before, one will become a madman, once one understands her. The robber has his hiding place by the noisy high-road, and the ant-lion his funnel in the loose sand, and the pirate his haunts by the roaring sea: likewise have I may fashion shop in the very midst of the teeming streets, seductive, irresistible to woman as is the Venusberg to men. There, in a fashion-shop, one learns to know woman, in a practical way and without any theoretical ado.

Now, if fashion meant nothing than that woman in the heat of her desire threw off all her clothing—why, then it would stand for something. But this is not the case, fashion is not plain sensuality, not tolerated debauchery, but an illicit trade in indecency authorized as proper. And, just as in heathen Prussia the marriageable girl wore a bell whose ringing served as a signal to the men, likewise is a woman's existence in fashion a continual bell-ringing, not for debauchees but for lickerish voluptuaries. People hold Fortune to be a woman—ah, yes it is, to be sure, fickle; still, it is fickle in something, as it may also give much; and insofar it is not a woman. No; but fashion is a woman, for fashion is fickleness in nonsense, and is consistent only in its becoming ever more crazy.

One hour in my shop is worth more than days and years without, if it really be one's desire to learn to know woman; in my shop, for it is the only one in the capital, there is no thought of competition. Who, forsooth, would dare to enter into competition with one who has entirely devoted himself, and is still devoting himself, as high-priest in this idol worship? No, there is not a distinguished assemblage which does not mention my name first and last; and there is not a Middle-class gathering where my name, whenever mentioned, does not inspire sacred awe, like that of the king; and there is no dress so idiotic but is accompanied by whistlers of admiration when its owner proceeds down the hall—provided it bears my name; and there is not the lady of gentle birth who dares pass my shop by, nor the girl of humble origin but passes it sighing and thinking: if only I could afford it! Well, neither was she deceived. I deceive no one; I furnish the finest goods and the most costly, and at the lowest price, indeed, I sell below cost. The fact is, I do not wish to make a profit. On the contrary, every year I sacrifice large sums. And yet do I mean to win, I mean to, I shall spend my last farthing in order to corrupt, in order to bribe, the tools of fashion so that I may win the game. To me it is a delight beyond compare to unroll the most precious stuffs, to cut them out, to clip pieces from genuine Brussels-lace, in order to make a fool's costume I sell to the lowest prices, genuine goods and in style.

You believe, perhaps, that woman wants to be dressed fashionably only at certain times? No such thing, she wants to be so all the time and that is her only thought. For a woman does have a mind, only it is employed about as well as is the Prodigal Son's substance; and woman does possess the power of reflection in an incredibly high degree, for there is nothing so holy but she will in no time discover it to be reconcilable with her finery—and the chiefest expression of finery is fashion. What wonder if she does discover it to be reconcilable; for is not fashion holy to her? And there is nothing so insignificant but she certainly will know how to make it count in her finery—and the most fatuous expression of finery is fashion. And there is nothing, nothing in all her attire, not the least ribbon, of whose relation to fashion she has not a definite conception and concerning which she is not immediately aware whether the lady who just passed by noticed it; because, for whose benefit does she dress, if not for other ladies!

Even in my shop where she comes to be fitted out à la mode, even there she is in fashion. Just as there is a special bathing costume and a special riding habit, likewise there is a particular kind of dress which it is the fashion to wear to the dressmaker's shop. That costume is not insouciant in the same sense as is the negligée a lady is pleased to be surprised in, earlier in the forenoon, where the point is her belonging to the fair sex and the coquetry lies in her letting herself be surprised. The dressmaker costume, on the other hand, is calculated to be nonchalant and a bit careless without her being embarrassed thereby; because a dressmaker stands in a different relation to her from a cavalier. The coquetry here consists in thus showing herself to a man who, by reason of his station, does not presume to ask for the lady's womanly recognition, but must be content with the perquisites which fall abundantly to his share, without her ever thinking of it; or without it even so much as entering her mind to play the lady before a dressmaker. The point is, therefore, that her being of the opposite sex is, in a certain sense, left out of consideration, and her coquetry invalidated, by the superciliousness of the noble lady who would smile if anyone alluded to any relation existing between her and her dressmaker. When visited in her negligée she conceals herself, thus displaying her charms by this very concealment. In my shop she exposes her charms with the utmost nonchalance, for he is only a dressmaker—and she is a woman. Now, her shawl slips down and bares some part of her body, and if I did not know what that means, and what she expects, my reputation would be gone to the winds. Now, she draws herself up, a priori fashion, now she gesticulates a posteriori; now, she sways to and fro in her hips; now, she looks at herself in the mirror and sees my admiring phiz behind her in the glass; now, she minces her words; now, she trips along with short steps; now, she hovers; now, she draws her foot after her in a slovenly fashion; now, she lets herself sink softly into an arm-chair, whilst I with humble demeanor offer her a flask of smelling salts and with my adoration assuage her agitation; now, she strikes after me playfully; now, she drops her handkerchief and, without as much as a single motion, lets her relaxed arm remain in its pendent position, whilst I bend down low to pick it up and return it to her, receiving a little patronizing nod as a reward. These are the ways of a lady of fashion when in my shop. Whether Diogenes[1] made any impression on the Woman who was praying in a somewhat unbecoming posture, when he asked her whether she did not believe the gods could see her from behind—that I do not know; but this I do know, that if I should say to her ladyship kneeling down in church: "The folds of your gown do not fall according to fashion," she would be more alarmed than if she had given offense to the gods. Woe to the outcast, the male Cinderella, who has not comprehended this! Pro dii immortales[2] what, pray, is a woman who is not in fashion; per deos obsecro,[3] and what when she is in fashion!

Whether all this is true? Well, make trial of it: let the swain, when his beloved one sinks rapturously on his breast, whispering unintelligibly: "thine forever," and hides her head on his bosom—let him but say to her: "My sweet Kitty, your coiffure is not at all in fashion."—Possibly, men don't give thought to this; but he who knows it, and has the reputation of knowing it, he is the most dangerous man in the kingdom. What blissful hours the lover passes with his sweetheart before marriage I do not know; but of the blissful hours she spends in my shop he hasn't the slightest inkling, either. Without my special license and sanction a marriage is null and void, anyway—or else an entirely plebeian affair. Let it be the very moment when they are to meet before the altar, let her step forward with the very best conscience in the world that everything was bought in my shop and tried on there—and now, if I were to rush up And exclaim: "But mercy! gracious lady, your myrtle wreath is all awry"—why, the whole ceremony might be postponed, for aught I know. But men do not suspect these things, one must be a dressmaker to know. So immense is the power of reflection needed to fathom a woman's thought that only a man who dedicates himself wholly to the task will succeed, and even then only if gifted to start with. Happy therefore the man who does not associate with any woman, for she is not his, anyway, even if, she be no other man's; for she is possessed by that phantom born of the unnatural intercourse of woman's reflection with itself, fashion. Do you see, for this reason should woman always swear by fashion—then were there some force in her oath; for after all, fashion is the thing she is always thinking of,

---

[1] See Diogenes Lærtios, VI, 37.
[2] By the immortal gods.
[3] I adjure you by the gods.

the only thing she can think together with, and into, everything. For instance, the glad message has gone forth from my shop to all fashionable ladies that fashion decrees the use of a particular kind of head-dress to be worn in church, and that this head-dress, again, must be somewhat different for High Mass and for the afternoon service. Now when the bells are ringing the carriage stops in front of my door. Her ladyship descends (for also this has been decreed, that no one can adjust that head-dress save I, the fashion-dealer), I rush out, making low bows, and lead her into my cabinet. And whilst she languishingly reposes I put everything in order. Now she is ready and has looked at herself in the mirror; quick as any messenger of the gods I hasten in advance, open the door of my cabinet with a bow, then hasten to the door of my shop and lay my arm on my breast, like some oriental slave; but encouraged by a gracious courtesy, I even dare to throw her an adoring and admiring kiss—now she is seated in her carriage—oh dear! she left her hymn book behind. I hasten out again and hand it to her through the carriage window, I permit myself once more to remind her to hold her head a trifle more to the right, and herself to arrange things, should her head-dress become a bit disordered when descending. She drives away and is edified.

You believe, perhaps, that it is only great ladies who worship fashion, but far from it! Look at my seamstresses for whose dress I spare no expense, so that the dogmas of fashion may be proclaimed most emphatically from my shop. They form a chorus of half-witted creatures, and I myself lead them on as high-priest, as a shining example, squandering all, solely in order to make all womankind ridiculous. For when a seducer makes the boast that every woman's virtue has its price, I do not believe him; but I do believe that every woman at an early time will be crazed by the maddening and defiling introspection taught her by fashion, which will corrupt her more thoroughly than being seduced. have made trial more than once. If not able to corrupt her myself I set on her a few of fashion's slaves of her own nation; for just as one may train rats to bite rats, likewise is the crazed woman's sting like that of the tarantula. And most especially dangerous is it when some man lends his help.

Whether I serve the Devil or God I do not know; but I am right, I shall be right, I will be, so long as I possess a single farthing, I will be until the blood spurts out of my fingers. The physiologist pictures the shape of woman to show the dreadful effects of wearing a corset, and beside it he draws a picture of her normal figure. That is all entirely correct, but only one of the drawings has the validity of truth: they all wear corsets. Describe, therefore, the miserable, stunted perversity of the fashion-mad woman, Describe the insidious introspection devouring her, and then describe the womanly modesty which least of all knows about itself—do so and you have judged woman, have in very truth passed terrible sentence on her. If ever I discover such a girl who is contented and demure and not yet corrupted by indecent intercourse with women—she shall fall nevertheless. I shall catch her in my toils, already she stands at the sacrificial altar, that is to say, in my shop. With the most scornful glance a haughty nonchalance can assume I measure her appearance, she perishes with fright; a peal of laughter from the adjoining room where sit my trained accomplices annihilates her. And afterwards, when I have gotten her rigged up à la mode and she looks crazier than a lunatic, as crazy as one who would not be accepted even in a lunatic asylum, then she leaves me in a state of bliss—no man, not even a god, were able to inspire fear in her; for is she not dressed in fashion?

Do you comprehend me now, do you comprehend why I call you fellow-conspirators, even though in a distant way? Do you now comprehend my conception of woman? Everything in life is a matter of fashion, the fear of God is a matter of fashion, and so are love, and crinolines, and a ring through the nose. To the utmost of my ability will I therefore come to the support of the exalted genius who wishes to laugh at the most ridiculous of all animals. If woman has reduced everything to a matter of fashion, then will I, with the help of fashion, prostitute her, as she deserves to be; I have no peace, I the dressmaker, my soul rages when I think of my task—she will yet be made to wear a ring through her nose. Seek therefore no sweetheart, abandon love as you would the most dangerous neighborhood; for the one whom you love would also be made to go with a ring through her nose.

Thereupon John, called the Seducer, spoke as follows:

(The Speech of John the Seducer)

My dear boon companions, is Satan plaguing you? For, indeed, you speak like so many hired mourners, your eyes are red with tears and not with wine. You almost move me to tears also, for an unhappy lover does have a miserable time of it in life. Hinc illae lacrimae.[1] I, however, am a happy lover, and my only wish is to remain so. Very possibly, that is one of the concessions to woman which Victor is so afraid of.

---

[1] Therefore those tears.

Why not? Let it be a concession! Loosening the lead foil of this bottle of champagne also is a concession; letting its foaming contents flow into my glass also is a concession; and so is raising it to my lips—now I drain it—concedo.[1] Now, however, it is empty, hence I need no more concessions. Just the same with girls. If some unhappy lover has bought his kiss too dearly, this proves to me only that he does not know, either how to take what is coming to him or how to do it. I never pay too much for this sort of thing—that is a matter for the girls to decide. What this signifies? To me it signifies the most beautiful, the most delicious, and well-nigh the most persuasive, argumentum ad hominem; but since every woman, at least once in her life, possesses this argumentative freshness I do not see any reason why I should not let myself be persuaded. Our young friend wishes to make this experience in his thought. Why not buy a cream puff and be content with looking at it? I mean to enjoy. No mere talk for me! Just as an old song has it about a kiss: es ist kaum zu sehn, es ist nur filr Lippen, die genau sich verstehn[2]—understand each other so exactly that any reflection about the matter is but an impertinence and a folly. He who is twenty and does not grasp the existence of the categorical imperative "enjoy thyself"—he is a fool; and he who does not seize the opportunity is and remains a Christianfelder.[3]

However, you all are unhappy lovers, and that is why you are not satisfied with woman as she is. The gods forbid! As she is she pleases me, just as she is. Even Constantin's category of "the joke" seems to contain a secret desire. I, on the other hand, I am gallant. And why not? Gallantry costs nothing and gives one all and is the condition for all, erotic pleasure. Gallantry is the Masonic language of the senses and of voluptuousness, between man and woman. It is a natural language, as love's language in general is. It consists not of sounds but of desires disguised and of ever changing wishes. That an unhappy lover may be ungallant enough to wish to convert his deficit into a draught payable in immortality—that I understand well enough. That is to say, I for my part do not understand it; for to me a woman has sufficient intrinsic value. I assure every woman of this, it is the truth; and at the same time it is certain that I am the only one who is not deceived by

---

[1] I concede.
[2] It can hardly be seen, it is but for lips which understand each other exactly.
[3] Christiansfeld, a town in South Jutland, was the seat of a colony of Herrhutian Pietists.

this truth. As to whether a despoiled woman is worth less than man—about that I find no information in my price list. I do not pick flowers already broken, I leave them to the married men to use for Shrove-tide decoration. Whether e. g. Edward, wishes to consider the matter again, and again fall in love with Cordelia,[1] or simply repeat the affair in his reflection —that is his own business. Why should I concern myself with other peoples' affairs! I explained to her at an earlier time what I thought of her; and, in truth, she convinced me, convinced me to my absolute satisfaction, that my gallantry was well applied.

Concedo. Concessi.[2] If I should meet with another Cordelia, why then I shall enact a comedy "Ring number 2."[3] But you are unhappy lovers and have conspired together, and are worse deceived than the girls, notwithstanding that you are richly endowed by nature. But decision—the decision of desire, is the most essential thing in life. Our young friend will always remain an onlooker. Victor is an unpractical enthusiast. Constantin has acquired his good sense at too great a cost; and the fashion dealer is a madman. Stuff and nonsense! With all four of you busy about one girl, nothing would come of it.

Let one have enthusiasm enough to idealize, taste enough to join in the clinking of glasses at the festive board of enjoyment, sense enough to break off—to break off absolutely, as does Death, madness enough to wish to enjoy all over again—if you have all that you will be the favorite of gods and girls.

But of what avail to speak here? I do not intend to make proselytes. Neither is this the place for that. To be sure I love wine, to be sure I love the abundance of a banquet—all that is good; but let a girl be my company, and then I shall be eloquent. Let then Constantin have my thanks for the banquet, and the wine, and the excellent appointments—the speeches, however, were but indifferent. But in order that things shall have a better ending I shall pronounce a eulogy on woman.

Just as he who is to speak in praise of the divinity must be inspired by the divinity to speak worthily, and must therefore be taught by the divinity as to what he shall say, Likewise he who would speak of women. For woman, even less than the divinity, is a mere figment of

---

[1] The reference is to the "Diary of the Seducer" (in "Either—Or," part I). Edward is the scorned lover of Cordelia who is seduced by John.
[2] I concede. I have conceded.
[3] Reference to a comedy by Farquhar, which enjoyed a moderate popularity in Copenhagen.

man's brain, a day-dream, or a notion that occurs to one and which one pay argue about pro et contra. Nay, one learns from woman alone what to say of her. And the more teachers one has had, the better. The first time one is a disciple, the next time one is already over the chief difficulties, just as one learns in formal and learned disputations how to use the last opponent's compliments against a new opponent. Nevertheless nothing is lost. For as little as a kiss is a mere sample of good things, and as little as an embrace is an exertion, just as little is this experience exhaustive. In fact it is essentially different from the mathematical proof of a theorem, which remains ever the same, even though other letters be substituted. This method is one befitting mathematics and ghosts, but not love and women, because each is a new proof, corroborating the truth of the theorem in a different manner. It is my joy that, far from being less perfect than man, the female sex is, on the contrary, the more perfect. I shall, however, clothe my speech in a myth; and I shall exult, on woman's account whom you have so unjustly maligned, if my speech pronounce judgment on your souls, if the enjoyment of her beckon you only to flee you, as did the fruits from Tantalus; because you have fled, and thereby insulted, woman. Only thus, forsooth, may she be insulted, even though she scorn it, and though punishment instantly falls on him who had the audacity. I, however, insult no one. That is but the notion of married men, and a slander; whereas, in reality, I respect her more highly than does the man she is married to.

Originally there was but one sex, so the Greeks relate, and that was man's. Splendidly endowed he was, so he did honor to the gods—so splendidly endowed that the same happened to them as sometimes happens to a poet who has expended all his energy on a poetic invention: they grew jealous of man. Ay, what is worse, they feared that he would not willingly bow under their yoke; they feared, though with small reason, that he might cause their very heaven to totter. Thus they had raised up a power they scarcely held themselves able to curb. Then there was anxiety and alarm in the council of the gods. Much had they lavished in their generosity on the creation of man; but all must be risked now, for reason of bitter necessity; for all was at stake—so the gods believed—and recalled he could not be, as a poet may recall his invention. And by force he could not be subdued, or else the gods themselves could have done so; but precisely of that they despaired. He would have to be caught and subdued, then, by a power weaker than his own and yet stronger—one strong enough to compel him. What a marvellous power this would have to be! However, necessity teaches even the gods to surpass themselves in inventiveness. They sought and they found. That power was woman, the marvel of creation, even in the eyes of the gods a greater marvel than man—a discovery which the gods in their näiveté could not help but applaud themselves for. What more can be said in her praise than that she was able to accomplish what even the gods did not believe themselves able to do; and what more can be said in her praise than that she did accomplish it! But how marvellous a creation must be hers to have accomplished it.

It was a ruse of the gods. Cunningly the enchantress was fashioned, for no sooner had she bewitched man than she changed and caught him in all the circumstantialities of existence. It was that the gods had desired. But what, pray, can be more delicious, or more entrancing and bewitching, than what the gods themselves contrived, when battling for their supremacy, as the only means of luring man? And most assuredly it is so, for woman is the only, and the most seductive, power in heaven and on earth. When compared with her in this sense man will indeed be found to be exceedingly imperfect.

And the stratagem of the gods was crowned with success; but not always. There have existed at all times some men—a few—who have detected the deception. They perceive well enough woman's loveliness—more keenly, indeed than the others—but they also suspect the real state of affairs. I call them erotic natures and count myself among them. Men call them seducers, woman has no name for them—such persons are to her unnameable. These erotic natures are the truly fortunate ones. They live more luxuriously than do the very gods, for they regale themselves with food more delectable than ambrosia, and they drink what is more delicious than nectar; they eat the most seductive invention of the gods' most ingenious thought, they are ever eating dainties set for a bait—ah, incomparable delight, ah, blissful fare—they are ever eating but the dainties set for a bait; and they are never caught. All other men greedily seize and devour it, like bumpkins eating their cabbage, and are caught. Only the erotic nature fully appreciates the dainties set out for bait—he prizes them infinitely. Woman divines this, and for that reason there is a secret understanding between him and her. But he knows also that she is a bait, and that secret he keeps to himself.

That nothing more marvellous, nothing more delicious, nothing more seductive, than woman can be devised, for that vouch the gods and their pressing need which heightened their powers of invention;

for that vouches also the fact that they risked all, and in shaping her moved heaven and earth.

I now forsake the myth. The conception "man" corresponds to his "idea." I can therefore, if necessary, think of an individual man as existing. The idea of woman, on the other hand, is so general that no one single woman is able to express it completely. She is not contemporaneous with man (and hence of less noble origin), but a later creation, though more perfect than he. Whether now the gods took some part from him whilst he slept, from fear of waking him by taking too much; or whether they bisected him and made woman out of the one half—at any rate it was man who was partitioned. Hence she is the equal of man only after this partition. She is a delusion and a snare, but is so only afterwards, and for him who is deluded. She is finiteness incarnate; but in her first stage she is finiteness raised to the highest degree in the deceptive infinitude of all divine and human illusions. Now, the deception does not exist—one instant longer, and one is deceived.

She is finiteness, and as such she is a collective: one woman represents all women. Only the erotic nature comprehends this and therefore knows how to love many without ever being deceived, sipping the while all the delights the cunning gods were able to prepare. For this reason, as I said, woman cannot be fully expressed by one formula, but is, rather, an infinitude of finalities. He who wishes to think her "idea" will have the same experience as he who gazes on a sea of nebulous shapes which ever form anew, or as he who is dazed by looking over the waves whose foamy crests ever mock one's vision; for her "idea" is but the workshop of possibilities. And to the erotic nature these possibilities are the everlasting reason for his worship.

So the gods created her delicate and ethereal as if out of the mists of the summer night, yet goodly like ripe fruit; light like a bird, though the repository of what attracts all the world—light because the play of the forces is harmoniously balanced in the invisible center of a negative relation;[1] slender in growth, with definite lines, yet her body sinuous with beautiful curves; perfect, yet ever appearing as if completed but now; cool, delicious, and refreshing like new-fallen snow, yet blushing in coy transparency; happy like some pleasantry which makes one forget all one's sorrow; soothing as being the end of desire,

---

[1] I.e., evidently, she does not exist because of herself; hence she is in a "negative" relation to herself. The center of this relation is "what attracts all the world."

and satisfying in herself being the stimulus of desire. And the gods had calculated that man, when first beholding her, would be amazed, as one who sees himself, though familiar with that sight—would stand in amaze as one who sees himself in the splendor of perfection—would stand in amaze as one who beholds what he did never dream he would, yet beholds what, it would seem, ought to have occurred to him before—sees what is essential to life and yet gazes on it as being the very mystery of existence. It is precisely this contradiction in his admiration which nurses desire to life, while this same admiration urges him ever nearer, so that he cannot desist from gazing, cannot desist from believing himself familiar with the sight, without really daring to approach, even though he cannot desist from desiring.

When the gods had thus planned her form they were seized with fear lest they might not have the wherewithal to give it existence; but what they feared even more was herself. For they dared not let her know how beautiful she was, apprehensive of having someone in the secret who might spoil their ruse. Then was the crowning touch given to their wondrous creation: they made her faultless; but they concealed all this from her in the nescience of her innocence, and concealed it doubly from her in the impenetrable mystery of her modesty. Now she was perfect, and victory certain. Inviting she had been before, but now doubly so through her shyness, and beseeching through her shrinking, and irresistible through herself offering resistance. The gods were jubilant. And no allurement has ever been devised in the world so great as is woman, and no allurement is as compelling as is innocence, and no temptation is as ensnaring as is modesty, and no deception is as matchless as is woman. She knows of nothing, still her modesty is instinctive divination. She is distinct from man, and the separating wall of modesty parting them is more decisive than Aladdin's sword separating him from Gulnare;[1] and yet, when like Pyramis he puts his head to this dividing wall of modesty, the erotic nature will perceive all pleasures of desire divined within as from afar.

Thus does woman tempt. Men are wont to set forth the most precious things they possess as a delectation for the gods, nothing less will do. Thus is woman a show-bread. the gods knew of naught comparable to her. She exists, she is present, she is with us, close by; and yet she is removed from us to an infinite distance when concealed in her modesty-until she herself betrays her hiding place, she knows not

---

[1] In Oehlenschläger's "Aladdin."

how: it is not she herself, it is life which informs on her. Roguish she is like a child who in playing peeps forth from his hiding place, yet her roguishness is inexplicable, for she does not know of it herself, she is ever mysterious-mysterious when she casts down her eyes, mysterious when she sends forth the messengers of her glance which no thought, let alone any word, is able to follow. And yet is the eye the "interpreter" of the soul! What, then, is the explanation of this mystery if the interpreter too is unintelligible? Calm she is like the hushed stillness of eventide, when not a leaf stirs; calm like a consciousness as yet unaware of aught. Her heart-beats are as regular as if life were not present; and yet the erotic nature, listening with his stethoscopically practiced ear, detects the dithyrambic pulsing of desire sounding along unbeknown. Careless she is like the blowing of the wind, content like the profound ocean, and yet full of longing like a thing biding its explanation. My friends! My mind is softened, indescribably softened. I comprehend that also my life expresses an idea, even if you do not comprehend me. I too have discovered the secret of existence; I too serve a divine idea—and, assuredly, I do not serve it for nothing. If woman is a ruse of the gods, this means that she is to be seduced; and if woman is not an "idea," the true inference is that the erotic nature wishes to love as many of them as possible.

What luxury it is to relish the ruse without being duped, only the erotic nature comprehends. And how blissful it is to be seduced, woman alone knows. I know that from woman, even though I never yet allowed any one of them time to explain it to me, but re-asserted my independence, serving the idea by a break as sudden as that caused by death; for a bride and a break are to one another like female and male.[1] Only woman is aware of this, and she is aware of it together with her seducer. No married man will ever grasp this. Nor does she ever speak with him about it. She resigns herself to her fate, she knows that it must be so and that she can be seduced only once. For this reason she never really bears malice against the man who seduced her. That is to say, if he really did seduce her and thus expressed the idea. Broken marriage vows and that kind of thing is, of course, nonsense and no seduction. Indeed, it is by no means so great a misfortune for a woman to be seduced. In fact, it is a piece of good fortune for her. An excellently seduced girl may make an excellent wife. If I myself were not fit to be a seducer—however deeply I feel my inferior qualifications in

---

[1] In the Danish, a pun on the hominyms en brud and et brud.

this respect—if I chose to be a married man, I should always choose a girl already seduced, so that I would not have to begin my marriage by seducing my wife. Marriage, to be sure, also expresses an idea; but in relation to the idea of marriage that quality is altogether immaterial which is the absolutely essential condition for my idea. Therefore, a marriage ought never to be planned to begin as though it were the beginning of a story of seduction. So much is sure: there is a seducer for every woman. Happy is she whose good fortune it is to meet just him.

Through marriage, on the other hand, the gods win their victory. In it the once seduced maiden walks through life by the side of her husband, looking back at times, full of longing, resigned to her fate, until she reaches the goal of life. She dies; but not in the same sense as man dies. She is volatilized and resolved into that mysterious primal element of which the gods formed her—she disappears like a dream, like an impermanent shape whose hour is past. For what is woman but a dream, and the highest reality withal! Thus does the erotic nature comprehend her, leading her, and being led by her in the moment of seduction, beyond time—where she has her true existence, being an illusion. Through her husband, on the other hand, she becomes a creature of this world, and he through her.

Marvellous nature! If I did not admire thee, a woman would teach me; for truly she is the venerable of life. Splendidly didst thou fashion her, but more splendidly still in that thou never didst fashion one woman like another. In man, the essential is the essential, and insofar always alike; but in woman the adventitious is the essential, and is thus an inexhaustible source of differences. Brief is her splendor; but quickly the pain is forgotten, too, when the same splendor is proffered me anew. It is true, I too am aware of the unbeautiful which may appear in her thereafter; but she is not thus with her seducer.

They rose from the table. It needed but a hint from Constantin, for the participants understood each other with military precision whenever there was a question of face or turn about. With his invisible baton of command, elastic like a divining rod in his hand, Constantin once more touched them in order to call forth in them a fleeting reminiscence of the banquet and the spirit of enjoyment which had prevailed before but was now, in some measure, submerged through the intellectual effort of the speeches— in order that the note of glad festivity which had disappeared might, by way of resonance, return once more among the guests in a brief moment of recollection. He saluted with his full glass as a signal of parting, emptying it, and then flinging it against the door in the rear wall. The others followed his example, consummating this symbolic action with all the solemnity of adepts. Justice was thus done the pleasure of stopping short—that royal pleasure which, though briefer, yet is more liberating than any other pleasure. With a libation this pleasure ought to be entered upon, with the libation of flinging one's glass into destruction and oblivion, and tearing one's self passionately away from every memory, as if it were a danger to one's life: this libation is to the gods of the nether world. One breaks off, and strength is needed to do that, greater strength than to sever a knot by a sword-blow; for the difficulty of the knot tends to arouse one's passion, but the passion required for breaking off must be of one's own making. In a superficial sense the result is, of course, the same; but from an artistic int of view there is a world of difference between something ceasing or simply coming to an end, and it being broken off by one's own free will—whether it is a mere occurrence or a passionate decision; whether it is all over, like a school song, because there is no more to it, or whether it is terminated by the Cæsarian operation of one's own Pleasure; whether it is a triviality everyone has experienced, or the secret which escapes most.

Constantin's flinging his beaker against the door was intended merely as a symbolic rite; nevertheless, his so doing was, in a way, a decisive act; for when the last glass was shattered the door opened, and just as he who presumptuously knocked at Death's door and, on its opening, beheld the powers of annihilation, so the banqueters beheld the corps of destruction ready to demolish everything—a memento which in an instant put them to flight from that place, while at the very same moment the entire surroundings had been reduced to the semblance of ruin.

A carriage stood ready at the door. At Constantin's invitation they seated themselves in it and drove away in good spirits; for that tableau of destruction which they left behind had given their souls fresh elasticity. After having covered a distance of several miles a halt was made. Here Constantin took his leave as host, informing them that five carriages were at their disposal—each one was free to suit his own pleasure and drive wherever he wanted, whether alone or in company with whomsoever he pleased. Thus a rocket, propelled by the force of the powder, ascends at a single shot, remains collected for an instant, in order then to spread out to all the winds.

While the horses were being hitched to the carriages the nocturnal banqueters strolled a little way down the road. The fresh air of the morning purified their hot blood with its coolness, and they gave themselves up to it entirely. Their forms, and the groups in which they ranged themselves, made a phantastic impression on me. For when the morning sun shines on field and meadow, and on every creature which in the night found rest and strength to rise up jubilating with the sun—in this there is only a pleasing, mutual understanding; but a nightly company, viewed by the morning light and in smiling surroundings, makes a downright uncanny impression. It makes one think of spooks which have been surprised by daylight, of subterranean spirits which are unable to regain the crevice through which they may vanish, because it is visible only in the dark; of unhappy creatures in whom the difference between day and night has become obliterated through the monotony of their sufferings.

A foot path led them through a small patch of field toward a garden surrounded by a hedge, from behind whose concealment a modest summer-cottage peeped forth. At the end of the garden, toward the field, there was an arbor formed by trees. Becoming aware of people being in the arbor, they all grew curious, and with the spying glances of men bent on observation, the besiegers closed in about that pleasant place of concealment, hiding themselves, and as eager as emissaries of the police about to take someone by surprise. Like emissaries of the police—well, to be sure, their appearance made the misunderstanding possible that it was they whom the minions of the law might be looking for. Each one had occupied a point of vantage for peeping in, when Victor drew back a step and said to his neighbor, "Why, dear me, if that is not Judge William and his wife!"

They were surprised—not the two whom the foliage concealed and who were all too deeply concerned with their domestic enjoyment to be observers. They felt themselves too secure to believe themselves an object of any one's observation excepting the morning sun's which took pleasure in looking in to them, whilst a gentle zephyr moved the boughs above them, and the reposefulness of the countryside, as well as all things around them girded the little arbor about with peace. The happy married couple was not surprised and noticed nothing. That they were a married couple was clear enough; one could perceive that at a glance—alas! if one is something of an observer one's self. Even if nothing in the wide world, nothing, whether overtly or covertly, if nothing, I say, threatens to interfere with the happiness of lovers, yet they are not thus secure when sitting together. They are in a state of bliss; and yet it is as if there were some power bent on separating them, so firmly they clasp one another; and yet it is as if there were some enemy present against whom they must defend themselves; ,and yet it is as if they could never become, sufficiently reassured. Not thus married people, and not thus that married couple in the arbor. How long they had been married, however, that was not to be determined with certainty. To be sure, the wife's activity at the tea-table revealed a sureness of hand born of practice, but at the same time such almost childlike interest in her occupation as if she were a newly married woman and in that middle condition when she is not, as yet, sure whether marriage is fun or earnest, whether being a housewife is a calling, or a game, or a pastime. Perhaps she had been married for some longer time but did not generally preside at the tea-table, or perhaps did so only out here in the country, or did it perhaps only that morning which, possibly, had a special significance for them. Who could tell? All calculation is frustrated to a certain degree by the fact that every personality exhibits some originality which keeps time from leaving its marks. When the sun shines in all his summer glory one thinks straightway that there must be some festal occasion at hand—that it cannot be so for every-day use, or that it is the first time, or at least one of the first times; for surely, one thinks, it cannot be repeated for any length of time. Thus would think he who saw it but once, or saw it for the first time; and I saw the wife of the justice for the first time. He who sees the object in question every day may think differently; provided he sees the same thing. But let the judge decide about that!

As I remarked, our amiable housewife was occupied. She poured boiling water into the cups, probably to warm them, emptied them again, set a cup on a platter, poured the tea and served it with sugar and cream—now all was ready; was it fun or earnest? In case a person did not relish tea at other times—he should have sat in the judge's place; for just then that drink seemed most inviting to me. only the inviting air of the lovely woman herself seemed to me more inviting.

It appeared that she had not had time to speak until then. Now she broke the silence and said, while serving him his tea: "Quick, now, dear, and drink while it is hot, the morning air is quite cool, anyway; and surely the least I can do for you is to be a little careful of you." "The least?" the judge answered laconically. "Yes, or the most, or the only thing." The judge looked at her inquiringly, and whilst he was helping himself she continued: "You interrupted me yesterday when I wished to broach the subject, but I have thought about it again; many times I have thought about it, and now particularly, you know yourself in reference to whom: it is certainly true that if you hadn't married, you would have been far more successful in your career." With his cup still on the platter the judge sipped a first mouthful with visible enjoyment, thoroughly refreshed; or was it perchance the joy over his lovely wife; I for my part believe it was the latter. She, however, seemed only to be glad that it tasted so good to him. Then he put down his cup on the table at his side, took out a cigar, and said: "May I light it at your chafing-dish"? "Certainly," she said, and handed him a live coal on a tea-spoon. He lit his cigar and put his arm about her waist whilst she leaned against his shoulder. He turned his head the other way to blow out the smoke and then he let his eyes rest on her with a devotion such as only a glance can reveal; yet he smiled, but this glad smile had in it a dash of sad irony. Finally he said: "Do you really believe so, my girl?" "What do you mean?" she answered. He was silent again, his smile gained the upper hand, but his voice remained quite serious, nevertheless. "Then I pardon you your previous folly, seeing that you yourself have forgotten it so quickly; thou speakest as one of the foolish women speaketh[1]—what great career should I have had?" His wife seemed embarrassed for a moment by this return, but collected her wits quickly and, now explained her meaning with womanly eloquence. The judge looked down before him, without interrupting her; but as she continued he began to drum on the table with the fingers of his right hand, at the same time humming a tune. The words of the song were audible for a moment, just as the pattern of a texture now becomes visible, now disappears again; and then again they were heard no longer as he hummed the tune of the song: "The goodman he went to the forest, to cut the wands so white." After this melodramatic performance, consisting in the justice's wife explaining herself whilst he hummed his tune, the dialogue set in again. "I am thinking," he remarked, "I am thinking you are ignorant of the fact that the Danish Law permits a man to castigate his wife[2] —a pity only that the law does not indicate on which occasions it is permitted." His wife smiled at his threat and continued: "Now why can I never get you to be serious when I touch on this matter? You do not understand me: believe me, I mean it sincerely, it seems to me a very beautiful thought. Of course, if you weren't my husband I would not dare to entertain it; but now I have done so, for your sake and for my sake; and now be nice

---

[1] Job 2,10.
[2] According to the Jutland Laws (A. D. 1241) a man is permitted to punish his wife, when she has misbehaved, with stick and with rod, but not with weapon. In the Danish Law (1683) this right is restricted to children and servants. S.V.

and serious, for my sake, and answer me frankly." "No, you can't get me to be serious, and a serious answer you won't get; I must either laugh at you, or make you forget it, as before, or beat you; or else you must stop talking, about it, or I shall have to make you keep silent about it some other way. You see, it is a joke, and that is why there are so many ways out." He arose, pressed a kiss on her brow, laid her arm in his, and then disappeared in a leafy walk which led from the arbor.

The arbor was empty; there was nothing else to do, so the hostile corps of occupation withdrew without making any gains. Still, the others were content with uttering some malicious remarks. The company returned but missed Victor. He had rounded the corner and, in walking along the garden, had come up to the country home. The doors of a garden-room facing the lawn were open, and likewise a window. Very probably he had seen something which attracted his attention. He leapt into the window, and leapt out again just as the party were approaching, for they had been looking for him. Triumphantly he held up some papers in his hand and exclaimed: "One of the judge's manuscripts![1] Seeing that I edited his other works it is no more than my duty that I should edit this one too." He put it into his pocket; or, rather, he was about to do so; for as he was bending his arm and already had his hand with the manuscript half-way down in his pocket I managed to steal it from him.

But who, then, am I? Let no one ask! If it hasn't occurred to you before to ask about it I am over the difficulty—for now the worst is behind me. For that matter, I am not worth asking about, for I am the least of all things, people would put me in utter confusion by asking about me. I am pure existence, and therefore smaller, almost, than nothing. I am "pure existence" which is present everywhere but still is never noticed; for I am ever vanishing. I am like the line above which stands the summa summarum—who cares about the line? By my own strength I can accomplish nothing, for even the idea to steal the manuscript from Victor was not my own idea; for this very idea which, as a thief would say, induced me to "borrow" the manuscript, was borrowed from him. And now, when editing, this manuscript, I am, again, nothing at all; for it rightly belongs to the judge. And as editor, I am in my nothingness only a kind of nemesis on Victor, who imagined that he had the prescriptive right to do so.

---

[1] Containing the second part of "Stages on Life's Road." entitled "Reflections on Marriage in Refutation of Objections."

Fear and Trembling

INTRODUCTION

Not only in the world of commerce but also in the world of ideas our age has arranged a regular clearance-sale. Everything may be had at such absurdly low prices that very soon the question will arise whether anyone cares to bid. Every waiter with a speculative turn who carefully marks the significant progress of modern philosophy, every lecturer in philosophy, every tutor, student, every sticker-and-quitter of philosophy—they are not content with doubting everything, but "go right on." It might, possibly, be ill-timed and inopportune to ask them whither they are bound; but it is no doubt polite and modest to take it for granted that they have doubted everything—else it were a curious statement for them to make, that they were proceeding onward. So they have, all of them, completed that preliminary operation and, it would seem, with such ease that they do not think it necessary to waste a word about how they did it. The fact is, not even he who looked anxiously and with a troubled spirit for some little point of information, ever found one, nor any instruction, nor even any little dietetic prescription, as to how one is to accomplish this enormous task. "But did not Descartes proceed in this fashion?" Descartes, indeed! that venerable, humble, honest thinker whose writings surely no one can read without deep emotion—Descartes did what he said, and said what he did. Alas, alas! that is a mighty rare thing in our times! But Descartes, as he says frequently enough, never uttered doubts concerning his faith. . . .

In our times, as was remarked, no one is content with faith, but "goes right on." The question as to whither they are proceeding may be a silly question; whereas it is, a sign of urbanity and culture to assume that everyone has faith, to begin with, for else it were a curious statement for them to make, that they are proceeding further. In the olden days it was different. Then, faith was a task for a whole life-time because it was held that proficiency in faith was not to be won within a few days or weeks. Hence, when the tried patriarch felt his end approaching, after having fought his battles and preserved his faith, he was still young enough at heart not to have forgotten the fear and trembling which disciplined his youth and which the mature man has under control, but which no one entirely outgrows—except insofar as he succeeds in "going on" as early as possible. The goal which those venerable men reached at last—at that spot everyone starts, in our times, in order to "proceed further.". . .

PREPARATION

There lived a man who, when a child, had heard the beautiful Bible story of how God tempted Abraham and how he stood the test, how he maintained his faith and, against his expectations, received his son back again. As this man grew older he read this same story with ever greater admiration; for now life had separated what had been united in the reverent simplicity of the child. And the older he grew, the more frequently his thoughts reverted to that story. His enthusiasm waxed stronger and stronger, and yet the story grew less and less clear to him. Finally he forgot everything else in thinking about it, and his soul contained but one wish, which was, to behold Abraham; and but one longing, which was, to have been witness to that event. His desire was, not to see the beautiful lands of the Orient, and not the splendor of the Promised Land, and not the reverent couple whose old age the Lord had blessed with children, and not the venerable figure of the aged patriarch, and not the god-given vigorous youth of Isaac—it would have been the same to him if the event had come to pass on some barren heath. But his wish was, to have been with Abraham on the three days' journey, when he rode with sorrow before him and with Isaac at his side. His wish was, to have been present at the moment when Abraham lifted up his eyes and saw Mount Moriah afar off; to have been present at the moment when he left his asses behind and wended his way up to the mountain alone with Isaac. For the mind of this man was busy, not with the delicate conceits of the imagination, but rather with his shuddering thought.

The man we speak of was no thinker, he felt no desire to go beyond his faith: it seemed to him the most glorious fate to be remembered as the Father of Faith, and a most enviable lot to be possessed of that faith, even if no one knew it.

The man we speak of was no learned exegetist, he did not even understand Hebrew—who knows but a knowledge of Hebrew might have helped him to understand readily both the story and Abraham.

I.

And God tempted Abraham and said unto him: take Isaac, thine only son, whom thou lovest and go to the land Moriah and sacrifice him there on a mountain which I shall show thee.[1]

It was in the early morning, Abraham arose betimes and had his asses saddled. He departed from his tent, and Isaac with him; but Sarah looked out of the window after them until they were out of sight. Silently they rode for three days; but on the fourth morning Abraham said not a word but lifted up his eyes and beheld Mount Moriah in the distance. He left his servants behind and, leading Isaac by the hand, he approached the mountain. But Abraham said to himself: "I shall surely conceal from Isaac whither he is going." He stood still, he laid his hand on Isaac's head to bless him, and Isaac bowed down to receive his blessing. And Abraham's aspect was fatherly, his glance was mild, his speech admonishing. But Isaac understood him not, his soul would not rise to him; he embraced Abraham's knees, he besought him at his feet, he begged for his young life, for his beautiful hopes, he recalled the joy in Abraham's house when he was born, he reminded him of the sorrow and the loneliness that would be after him. Then did Abraham raise up the youth and lead him by his hand, and his words were full of consolation and admonishment. But Isaac understood him not. He ascended Mount Moriah, but Isaac understood him not. Then Abraham averted his face for a moment; but when Isaac looked again, his father's countenance was changed, his glance wild, his aspect terrible, he seized Isaac and threw him to the ground and said: "Thou foolish lad, believest thou I am thy father? An idol-worshipper am I. Believest thou it is God's command? Nay, but my pleasure." Then Isaac trembled and cried out in his fear: "God in heaven, have pity on me, God of

---

[1] Freely after Genesis 22.

Abraham, show mercy to me, I have no father on earth, be thou then my father!" But Abraham said softly to himself: "Father in heaven, I thank thee. Better is it that he believes me inhuman than that he should lose his faith in thee."

When the child is to be weaned, his mother blackens her breast; for it were a pity if her breast should look sweet to him when he is not to have it. Then the child believes that her breast has changed; but his mother is ever the same, her glance is full of love and as tender as ever. Happy he who needed not worse means to wean his child!

II.

It was in the early morning. Abraham arose betimes and embraced Sarah, the bride of his old age. And Sarah kissed Isaac who had taken the shame from her—Isaac, her pride, her hope for all coming generations. Then the twain rode silently along their way, and Abraham's glance was fastened on the ground before him; until on the fourth day, when he lifted up his eyes and beheld Mount Moriah in the distance; but then his eyes again sought the ground. Without a word he put the fagots in order and bound Isaac, and without a word he unsheathed his knife. Then he beheld the ram God had chosen, and sacrificed him, and wended his way home.... From that day on Abraham grew old. He could not forget that God had required this of him. Isaac flourished as before; but Abraham's eye was darkened, he saw happiness no more.

When the child has grown and is to be weaned, his mother will in maidenly fashion conceal her breast. Then the child has a mother no longer. Happy the child who lost not his mother in any other sense!

III.

It was in the early morning. Abraham arose betimes he kissed Sarah, the young mother, and Sarah kissed Isaac, her joy, her delight for all times. And Abraham rode on his way, lost in thought—he was thinking of Hagar and her son whom he had driven out into the wilderness. He ascended Mount Moriah and he drew the knife.

It was a calm evening when Abraham rode out alone, and he rode to Mount Moriah. There he cast himself down on his face and prayed to God to forgive him his sin in that he had been about to sacrifice his son Isaac, and in that the father had forgotten his duty toward his son. And yet oftener he rode on his lonely way, but he found no rest. He could not grasp that it was a sin that he had wanted to sacrifice to God his most precious possession, him for whom he would most gladly have died many times. But, if it was a sin, if he had not loved Isaac thus, then could he not grasp the possibility that he could be forgiven : for what sin more terrible ?

When the child is to be weaned, the mother is not without sorrow that she and her child are to be separated more and more, that the child who had first lain under her heart, and afterwards at any rate rested at her breast, is to be so near to her no more. So they sorrow together for that brief while. Happy he who kept his child so near to him and needed not to sorrow more!

IV.

It was in the early morning. All was ready for the journey in the house of Abraham. He bade farewell to Sarah; and Eliezer, his faithful servant, accompanied him along the way for a little while. They rode together in peace, Abraham and Isaac, until they came to Mount Moriah. And Abraham prepared everything for the sacrifice, calmly and mildly; but when his father turned aside in order to unsheathe his knife, Isaac saw that Abraham's left hand was knit in despair and that a trembling shook his frame—but Abraham drew forth the knife.

Then they returned home again, and Sarah hastened to meet them; but Isaac had lost his faith, No one in all the world ever said a word about this, nor did Isaac speak to any man concerning what he had seen, and Abraham suspected not that anyone had seen it.

When the child is to be weaned, his mother has the stronger food ready lest the child perish. Happy he who has in readiness this stronger food!

Thus, and in many similar ways, thought the man whom I have mentioned about this event. And every time he returned, after a pilgrimage to Mount Moriah, he sank down in weariness, folding his hands and saying: "No one, in truth, was great as was Abraham, and who can understand him?"

A PANEGYRIC ON ABRAHAM

If a consciousness of the eternal were not implanted in man; if the basis of all that exists were but a confusedly fermenting element which, convulsed by obscure passions, Produced all, both the great and the insignificant; if under everything there lay a bottomless void never to be filled what else were life but despair? If it were thus, and if there were no sacred bonds between man and man; if one generation arose after another, as in the forest the leaves of one season succeed the leaves of another, or like the songs of birds which are taken up one after another; if the generations of man passed through the world like a ship passing through the sea and the wind over the desert—a fruitless and a vain thing; if eternal oblivion were ever greedily watching for its prey and there existed no power strong enough to wrest it from its clutches—how empty were life then, and how dismal! And therefore it is not thus; but, just as God created man and woman, he likewise called into being the hero and the poet or orator. The latter cannot perform the deeds of the hero—he can only admire and love him and rejoice in him. And yet he also is happy and not less so; for the hero is, as it were, his better self with which he has fallen in love, and he is glad he is not himself the hero, so that his love can express itself in admiration.

The poet is the genius of memory, and does nothing but recall what has been done, can do nothing but admire what has been done. He adds nothing of his own, but he is Jealous of what has been entrusted to him. He obeys the choice of his own heart; but once he has found what he has been seeking, he visits every man's door with his song and with his speech, so that all may admire the hero as he does, and be proud of the hero as he is. This is his achievement, his humble work, this is his faithful service in the house of the hero. If thus, faithful to his love, he battles day and night against the guile of oblivion which wishes to lure the hero from him, then has he accomplished his task, then is he gathered to his hero who loves him as faithfully; for the poet is as it were the hero's better self, unsubstantial, to be sure, like a mere memory, but also transfigured as is a memory. Therefore shall no one be forgotten who has done great deeds; and even if there be delay, even if the cloud of misunderstanding obscure the hero from our vision, still his lover will come sometime; and the more time has passed, the more faithfully will he cleave to him.

No, no one shall be forgotten who was great in this world. But each hero was great in his own way, and each one was eminent in proportion to the great things he loved. For he who loved himself became great through himself, and he who loved others became great through his devotion, but he who loved God became greater than all of these. Every one of them shall be remembered, but each one became great in proportion to his trust. One became great by the possible; another, by hoping for the eternal; hoped for the impossible, he became greater than all of these. Every one shall be remembered; but each one was great in proportion to the power with which he strove. For he who strove with the world became great by overcoming himself; but he who strove with God, he became the greatest of them all. Thus there have been struggles in the world, man against man, one against a thousand; but he who struggled with God, he became greatest of them all. Thus there was fighting on this earth, and there was he who conquered everything by his strength, and there was he who conquered God by his weakness. There was he who, trusting in himself, gained all; and there was he who, trusting in his strength sacrificed everything; but he who believed in God was greater than all of these. There was he who was great through his strength, and he who was great through his wisdom, and he who was great through his hopes, and he who was great through his love; but Abraham was greater than all of these—great through the strength whose power is weakness, great through the wisdom whose secret is folly, great through the hope whose expression is madness, great through the love which is hatred of one's self.

Through the urging of his faith Abraham left the land of his forefathers and became a stranger in the land of promise. He left one thing behind and took one thing along: he left his worldly wisdom behind and took with him faith. For else he would not have left the land of his fathers. but would have thought it an unreasonable demand. Through his faith he came to be a stranger in the land of promise, where there was nothing to remind him of all that had been dear to him, but where everything by its newness tempted his soul to longing. And yet was he God's chosen, he in whom the Lord was well pleased! Indeed, had he been one cast off, one thrust out of God's mercy, then might he have comprehended it; but now it seemed like a mockery of him and of his faith. There have been others who lived in exile from the fatherland which they loved. They are not forgotten, nor is the song of lament forgotten in which they mournfully sought and found what they had lost. Of Abraham there exists no song of lamentation. It is human to complain, it is human to weep with the weeping; but it is greater to believe, and more blessed to consider him who has faith.

Through his faith Abraham received the promise that in his seed were to be blessed all races of mankind. Time passed, there was still the possibility of it, and Abraham had faith. Another man there was who also lived in hopes. Time passed, the evening of his life was approaching; neither was he paltry enough to have forgotten his hopes: neither shall he be forgotten by us! Then he sorrowed, and his sorrow did not deceive him, as life had done, but gave him all it could; for in the sweetness of sorrow he became possessed of his disappointed hopes. It is human to sorrow, it is human to sorrow with the sorrowing; but it is greater to have faith, and more blessed to consider him who has faith.

No song of lamentation has come down to us from Abraham. He did not sadly count the days as time passed; he did not look at Sarah with suspicious eyes, whether she was becoming old; he did not stop the sun's course lest Sarah should grow old and his hope with her; he did not lull her with his songs of lamentation. Abraham grew old, and Sarah became a laughing-stock to the people; and yet was he God's chosen, and heir to the promise that in his seed were to be blessed all races of mankind. Were it, then, not better if he had not been God's chosen? For what is it to be God's chosen? Is it to have denied to one in one's youth all the wishes of youth in order to have them fulfilled after great labor in old age?

But Abraham had faith and steadfastly lived in hope. Had Abraham been less firm in his trust, then would he have given up that hope. He would have said to God: "So it is, perchance, not Thy will, after all, that this shall come to pass. I shall surrender my hope. It was my only one, it was my bliss. I am sincere, I conceal no secret grudge for that Thou didst deny it to me." He would not have remained forgotten, his example would have saved many a one; but he would not have become the Father of Faith. For it is great to surrender one's hope, but greater still to abide by it steadfastly after having surrendered it; for it is great to seize hold of the eternal hope, but greater till to abide steadfastly by one's worldly hopes after having rendered them.

Then came the fullness of time. If Abraham had not had faith, then Sarah would probably have died of sorrow, and Abraham, dulled by his grief, would not have understood the fulfillment, but would have smiled about it as a dream of his youth. But Abraham had faith, and therefore he remained young; for he who always hopes for the best, him life will deceive, and he will grow old; and he who is always prepared for the worst, he will soon age; but he who has faith, he will preserve eternal youth. Praise, therefore, be to this story! For Sarah, though advanced in age, was young enough to wish for the pleasures of a mother, and Abraham, though grey of hair, was young enough to wish to become a father. In a superficial sense it may be considered miraculous that what they wished for came to pass, but in a deeper sense the miracle of faith is to be seen in Abraham's and Sarah's being young enough to wish, and their faith having preserved their wish and therewith their youth. The promise he had received was fulfilled, and he accepted it in faith, and it came to pass according to the promise and his faith; whereas Moses smote the rock with his staff but believed not.

There was joy in Abraham's house when Sarah celebrated the day of her Golden Wedding. But it was not to remain thus; for once more was Abraham to be tempted. He had struggled with that cunning power to which nothing is impossible, with that ever watchful enemy who never sleeps, with that old man who outlives all—he had struggled with Time and had preserved his faith. And now all the terror of that fight was concentrated in one moment. "And God tempted Abraham, saying to him: take now thine only son Isaac, whom thou lovest, and get thee into the land of Moriah; and offer him there for a burnt offering upon one of the mountains which I will tell thee of.[1]

All was lost, then, and more terribly than if a son had never been given him! The Lord had only mocked Abraham, then! Miraculously he had realized the unreasonable hopes of Abraham; and now he wished to take away what he had given. A foolish hope it had been, but Abraham had not laughed when the promise had been made him. Now all was lost—the trusting hope of seventy years, the brief joy at the fulfillment of his hopes. Who, then, is he that snatches away the old man's staff, who that demands that he himself shall break it in two? Who is he that renders disconsolate the grey hair of old age, who is he that demands that he himself shall do it? Is there no pity for the venerable old man, and none for the innocent child? And yet was Abraham God's chosen one, and yet was it the Lord that tempted him. And now all was to be lost I The glorious remembrance of him by a whole race, the promise of Abraham's seed-all that was but a whim, a passing fancy of the Lord, which Abraham was now to destroy forever! That glorious treasure, as old as the faith in Abraham's heart, and many, many years older than Isaac, the fruit of Abraham's life, sanctified by prayers, matured in struggles—the blessing on the lips of Abraham:

---

[1] Genesis 20, 11 f.

this fruit was now to be plucked before the appointed time, and to remain without significance; for of what significance were it if Isaac was to be sacrificed? That sad and yet blessed hour when Abraham was to take leave from all that was dear to him, the hour when he would once more lift up his venerable head, when his face would shine like the countenance of the Lord, the hour when he would collect his whole soul for a blessing strong enough to render Isaac blessed all the days, of his life-that hour was not to come! He was to say farewell to Isaac, to be sure, but in such wise that he himself was to remain behind; death was to part them, but in such wise that Isaac was to die. The old man was not in happiness to lay his hand on Isaac's head when the hour of death came, but, tired of life, to lay violent hands on Isaac. And it was God who tempted him. Woe, woe to the messenger who would have come before Abraham with such a command! Who would have dared to be the messenger of such dread tidings? But it was God that tempted Abraham.

But Abraham had faith, and had faith for this life. Indeed, had his faith been but concerning the life to come, then might he more easily have cast away all, in order to hasten out of this world which was not his. . . .

But Abraham had faith and doubted not, but trusted that the improbable would come to pass. If Abraham had doubted, then would he have undertaken something else, something great and noble; for what could Abraham have undertaken but was great and noble! He would have proceeded to Mount Moriah, he would have cloven the wood, and fired it, and unsheathed his knife—he would have cried out to God: "Despise not this sacrifice; it is not, indeed, the best I have; for what is an old man against a child foretold of God; but it is the best I can give thee. Let Isaac never know that he must find consolation in his youth." He would have plunged the steel in his own breast. And he would have been admired throughout the world, and his name would not have been forgotten; but it is one thing to be admired and another, to be a lode-star which guides one troubled in mind.

But Abraham had faith. He prayed not for mercy and that he might prevail upon the Lord: it was only when just retribution was to be visited upon Sodom and Gomorrha that Abraham ventured to beseech Him for mercy.

Søren Kierkegaard

We read in Scripture: "And God did tempt Abraham, and said unto him, Abraham: and he said, Behold here I am."[1] You, whom I am now addressing did you do likewise? When you saw the dire dispensations of Providence approach threateningly, did you not then say to the mountains, Fall on me; and to the hills, Cover me?[2] Or, if you were stronger in faith, did not your step linger along the way, longing for the old accustomed paths, as it were? And when the voice called you, did you answer, then, or not at all, and if you did, perchance in a low voice, or whispering? Not thus Abraham, but gladly and cheerfully and trustingly, and with a resonant voice he made answer: "Here am I" And we read further: "And Abraham rose up early in the morning.[3] He made haste as though for some joyous occasion, and early in the morning he was in the appointed place, on Mount Moriah. He said nothing to Sarah, nothing to Eliezer, his steward; for who would have understood him? Did not his temptation by its very nature demand of him the vow of silence? "He laid the wood in order, and bound Isaac his son, and laid him on the altar upon the wood. And Abraham stretched forth his hand, and took the knife to slay his son." My listener! Many a father there has been who thought that with his child he lost the dearest of all there was in the world for him; yet assuredly no child ever was in that sense a pledge of God as was Isaac to Abraham. Many a father there has been who lost his child; but then it was God, the unchangeable and inscrutable will of the Almighty and His hand which took it. Not thus with Abraham. For him was reserved a more severe trial, and Isaac's fate was put into Abraham's hand together with the knife. And there he stood, the old man, with his only hope! Yet did he not doubt, nor look anxiously to the left or right, nor challenge Heaven with his prayers. He knew it was God the Almighty who now put him to the test; he knew it was the greatest sacrifice which could be demanded of him; but he knew also that no sacrifice was too great which God demanded—and he drew forth his knife.

Who strengthened Abraham's arm, who supported his right arm that it drooped not powerless? For he who contemplates this scene is unnerved. Who strengthened Abraham's soul so that his eyes grew not too dim to see either Isaac or the ram? For he who contemplates this scene will be struck with blindness. And yet, it is rare enough that one

---

[1] Genesis 22,1.
[2] Luke 23, 30.
[3] Genesis 22, 3 and 9.

is unnerved or is struck with blindness, and still more rare that one narrates worthily what there did take place between father and son. To be sure, we know well enough—it was but a trial!

If Abraham had doubted, when standing on Mount Moriah; if he had looked about him in perplexity; if he had accidentally discovered the ram before drawing his knife; if God had permitted him to sacrifice it instead of Isaac—then would he have returned home, and all would have been as before, he would have had Sarah and would have kept Isaac; and yet how different all would have been! For then had his return been a flight, his salvation an accident, his reward disgrace, his future, perchance, perdition. Then would he have borne witness neither to his faith nor to God's mercy, but would have witnessed only to the terror of going to Mount Moriah. Then Abraham would not have been forgotten, nor either Mount Moriah. It would be mentioned, then, not as is Mount Ararat on which the Ark landed, but as a sign of terror, because it was there Abraham doubted.

Venerable patriarch Abraham! When you returned home from Mount Moriah you required no encomiums to console you for what you had lost; for, indeed, you did win all and still kept Isaac, as we all know. And the Lord did no more take him from your side, but you sate gladly at table with him in your tent as in the life to come you will, for all times. Venerable patriarch Abraham! Thousands of years have passed since those times, but still you need no late-born lover to snatch your memory from the power of oblivion, for every language remembers you—and yet do you reward your lover more gloriously than anyone, rendering him blessed in your bosom, and taking heart and eyes captive by the marvel of your deed. Venerable patriarch Abraham! Second father of the race! You who first perceived and bore witness to that unbounded passion which has but scorn for the terrible fight with the raging elements and the strength of brute creation, in order to struggle with God; you who first felt that sublimest of all passions, you who found the holy, pure, humble expression for the divine madness which was a marvel to the heathen—forgive him who would speak in your praise, in case he did it not fittingly. He spoke humbly, as if it concerned the desire of his heart; he spoke briefly, as is seemly; but he will never forget that you required a hundred years to obtain a son of your old age, against all expectations; that you had to draw the knife before being permitted to keep Isaac; he will never forget that in a hundred and thirty years you never got farther than to faith.

Søren Kierkegaard

PRELIMINARY EXPECTORATION

An old saying, derived from the world of experience, has it that "he who will not work shall not eat.¹ But, strange to say, this does not hold true in the world where it is thought applicable; for in the world of matter the law of imperfection prevails, and we see, again and again, that he also who will not work has bread to eat—indeed, that he who sleeps has a greater abundance of it than he who works. In the world of matter everything belongs to whosoever happens to possess it; it is thrall to the law of indifference, and he who happens to possess the Ring also has the Spirit of the Ring at his beck and call, whether now he be Noureddin or Aladdin² and he who controls the treasures of this world, controls them, howsoever he managed to do so. It is different in the world of spirit. There, an eternal and divine order obtains, there the rain does not fall on the just and the unjust alike, nor does the sun shine on the good and the evil alike;³ but there the saying does hold true that he who will not work shall not eat, and only he who was troubled shall find rest, and only he who descends into the nether world shall rescue his beloved, and only he who unsheathes his knife shall be given Isaac again. There, he who will not work shall not eat, but shall be deceived, as the gods deceived Orpheus with an immaterial figure instead of his beloved Euridice,⁴ deceived him because he was love-sick and not courageous, deceived him because he was a player on the cithara rather than a man.. There, it avails not to have an Abraham for one's father,⁵ or to have seventeen ancestors. But in that world the saying about Israel's maidens will hold true of him who will not work: he shall bring forth wind;⁶ but he who will work shall give birth to his own father.

There is a kind of learning which would presumptuously introduce into the world of spirit the same law of indifference under which the world of matter groans. It is thought that to know about great men and

---

¹ Cf. Thessalonians 3, 10.
² In Aladin, Oehlenschläger's famous dramatic poem, Aladdin, "the cheerful son of nature," is contrasted with Noureddin, representing the gloom of doubt and night.
³ Matthew 5, 45.
⁴ Cf. not the legend but Plato's Symposium.
⁵ Matthew 3, 9.
⁶ Isaiah 26, 18.

great deeds is quite sufficient, and that other exertion is not necessary. And therefore this learning shall not eat, but shall perish of hunger while seeing all things transformed into gold by its touch. And what, forsooth, does this learning really know? There were many thousands of contemporaries, and countless men in after times, who knew all about the triumphs of Miltiades; but there was only one whom they rendered sleepless.[1] There have existed countless generations that knew by heart, word for word, the story of Abraham; but how many has it rendered sleepless?

Now the story of Abraham has the remarkable property of always being glorious, in however limited a sense it is understood; still, here also the point is whether one means to labor and exert one's self. Now people do not care to labor and exert themselves, but wish nevertheless to understand the story. They extol Abraham, but how? By expressing the matter in the most general terms and saying: "the great thing about him was that he loved God so ardently that he was willing to sacrifice to Him his most precious possession." That is very true; but "the most precious possession" is an indefinite expression. As one's thoughts, and one's mouth, run on one assumes, in a very easy fashion, the identity of Isaac and "the most precious possession"—and meanwhile he who is meditating may smoke his pipe, and his audience comfortably stretch out their legs. If the rich youth whom Christ met on his way[2] had sold all his possessions and given all to the poor, we would extol him as we extol all which is great—aye, would not understand even him without labor; and yet would he never have become an Abraham, notwithstanding his sacrificing the most precious possessions he had. That which people generally forget in the story of Abraham is his fear and anxiety; for as regards money, one is not ethically responsible for it, whereas for his son a father has the highest and most sacred responsibility. However, fear is a dreadful thing for timorous spirits, so they omit it. And yet they wish to speak of Abraham.

So they keep on speaking, and in the course of their speech the two terms Isaac and "the most precious thing" are used alternately, and everything is in the best order. But now suppose that among the audience there was a man who suffered with sleeplessness—and then the most terrible and profound, the most tragic, and at the same time the, most comic, misunderstanding is within the range of possibility. That

---

[1] Themistocles, that is; see Plutarch, Lives.
[2] Matthew 19,16f.

is, suppose this man goes home and wishes to do as did Abraham; for his son is his most precious possession. If a certain preacher learned of this he would, perhaps, go to him, he would gather up all his spiritual dignity and exclaim: "'Thou abominable creature, thou scum of humanity, what devil possessed thee to wish to murder son?" And this preacher, who had not felt any particular warmth, nor perspired while speaking about Abraham, this preacher would be astonished himself at the earnest wrath with which he poured forth his thunders against that poor wretch; indeed, he would rejoice over himself, for never had he spoken with such power and unction, and he would have said to his wife: "I am an orator, the only thing I have lacked so far was the occasion. Last Sunday, when speaking about Abraham, I did not feel thrilled in the least."

Now, if this same orator had just a bit of sense to spare, I believe he would lose it if the sinner would reply, in a quiet and dignified manner: "Why, it was on this very same matter you preached, last Sunday!" But however could the preacher have entertained such thoughts? Still, such was the case, and the preacher's mistake was merely not knowing what he was talking about. Ah, would that some poet might see his way clear to prefer such a situation to the stuff and nonsense of which novels and comedies are full! For the comic and the tragic here run parallel to infinity. The sermon probably was ridiculous enough in itself, but it became infinitely ridiculous through the very natural consequence it had. Or, suppose now the sinner was converted by this lecture without daring to raise any objection, and this zealous divine now went home elated, glad in the consciousness of being effective, not only in the pulpit, but chiefly, and with irresistible power, as a spiritual guide, inspiring his congregation on Sunday, whilst on Monday he would place himself like a cherub with flaming sword before the man who by his actions tried to give the lie to the old saying that "the course of the world follows not the priest's word."

If, on the other hand, the sinner were not convinced of his error his position would become tragic. He would probably be executed, or else sent to the lunatic asylum—at any rate, he would become a sufferer in this world; but in another sense I should think that Abraham rendered him happy; for he who labors, he shall not perish.

Now how shall we explain the contradiction contained in that sermon? Is it due to Abraham's having the reputation of being a great man—so that whatever he does is great, but if another should undertake to do the same it is a sin, a heinous sin ? If this be the case I prefer not to participate in such thoughtless laudations. If faith cannot make it a sacred thing to wish to sacrifice one's son, then let the same judgment be visited on Abraham as on any other man. And if we perchance lack the courage to drive our thoughts to the logical conclusion and to say that Abraham was a murderer, then it were better to acquire that courage, rather than to waste one's time on undeserved encomiums. The fact is, the ethical expression for what Abraham did is that he wanted to murder Isaac; the religious, that he wanted to sacrifice him. But precisely in this contradiction is contained the fear which may well rob one of one's sleep. And yet Abraham were not Abraham without this fear. Or, again, supposing Abraham did not do what is attributed to him, if his action was an entirely different one, based on conditions of those times, then let us forget him; for what is the use of calling to mind that past which can no longer become a present reality?—Or, the speaker had perhaps forgotten the essential fact that Isaac was the son. For if faith is eliminated, having been reduced to a mere nothing, then only the brutal fact remains that Abraham wanted to murder Isaac—which is easy for everybody to imitate who has not the faith—the faith, that is, which renders it most difficult for him. . . .

Love has its priests in the poets, and one bears at times a poet's voice which worthily extols it. But not a word does one hear of faith. Who is there to speak in honor of that passion? Philosophy "goes right on." Theology sits at the window with a painted visage and sues for philosophy's favor, offering it her charms. It is said to be difficult to understand the philosophy of Hegel; but to understand Abraham, why, that is an easy matter! To proceed further than Hegel is a wonderful feat, but to proceed further than Abraham, why, nothing is easier! Personally, I have devoted a considerable amount of time to a study of Hegelian philosophy and believe I understand it fairly well; in fact, I am rash enough to say that when, notwithstanding an effort, I am not able to understand him in some passages, is because he is not entirely clear about the matter himself. All this intellectual effort I perform easily and naturally, and it does not cause my head to ache. On the other hand, whenever I attempt to think about Abraham I am, as it were, overwhelmed. At every moment I am aware of the enormous paradox which forms the content of Abraham's life, at every moment I am repulsed, and my thought, notwithstanding its passionate attempts, cannot penetrate into it, cannot forge on the breadth of a hair. I strain every muscle in order to envisage the problem—and become a paralytic in the same moment.

I am by no means unacquainted with what has been admired as great and noble, my soul feels kinship with it, being satisfied, in all humility, that it was also may cause the hero espoused; and when contemplating his deed I say to myself: "jam tua causa agitur."[1] I am able to identify myself with the hero; but I cannot do so with Abraham, for whenever I have reached his height I fall down again, since he confronts me as the paradox. It is by no means my intention to maintain that faith is something inferior, but, on the contrary, that it is the highest of all things; also that it is dishonest in philosophy to offer something else instead, and to pour scorn on faith; but it ought to understand its own nature in order to know what it can offer. It should take away nothing; least of all, fool people out of something as if it were of no value. I am not unacquainted with the sufferings and dangers of life, but I do not fear them, and cheerfully go forth to meet them. . . . But my courage is not, for all that, the courage of faith, and is as nothing compared with it. I cannot carry out the movement of faith: I cannot close my eyes and confidently plunge into the absurd—it is impossible for me; but neither do I boast of it. . .

Now I wonder if every one of my contemporaries is really able to perform the movements of faith. Unless I am much mistaken they are, rather, inclined to be proud of making what they perhaps think me unable to do, viz., the imperfect movement. It is repugnant to my soul to do what is so often done, to speak inhumanly about great deeds, as if a few thousands of years were an immense space of time. I prefer to speak about them in a human way and as though they had been done but yesterday, to let the great deed itself be the distance which either inspires or condemns me. Now if I, in the capacity of tragic hero—for a higher flight I am unable to take—if I had been summoned to such an extraordinary royal progress as was the one to Mount Moriah, I know very well what I would have done. I would not have been craven enough to remain at home; neither would I have dawdled on the way; nor would I have forgot my knife—just to draw out the end a bit. But I am rather sure that I would have been promptly on the spot, with everything in order—in fact, would probably have been there before the appointed time, so as to have the business soon over with. But I know also what I would have done besides. In the moment I mounted my horse I would have said to myself: "Now all is lost, God demands Isaac, I shall sacrifice him, and with him all my joy—but for all that, God is love and will remain so for me; for in this world God and I cannot speak together, we have no language in common."

---

[1] Your cause, too, is at stake.

Possibly, one or the other of my contemporaries will be stupid enough, and jealous enough of great deeds, to wish to persuade himself and me that if I had acted thus I should have done something even greater than what Abraham did; for my sublime resignation was (he thinks) by far more ideal and poetic than Abraham's literal-minded action. And yet this is absolutely not so, for my sublime resignation was only a substitute for faith. I could not have made more than the infinite movement (of resignation) to find myself and again repose in myself. Nor would I have loved Isaac as Abraham loved him. The fact that I was resolute enough to resign is sufficient to prove my courage in a human sense, and the fact that I loved him with my whole heart is the very presupposition without which my action would be n. me; but still I did not love as did Abraham, for else I would have hesitated even in the last minute, without, for that matter, arriving too late on Mount Moriah. Also, I would have spoiled the whole business by my behavior; for if I had had Isaac restored to me I would have been embarrassed. That which was an easy matter for Abraham would have been difficult for me, I mean, to rejoice again in Isaac; for he who with all the energy of his soul proprio motu et propriis auspiciis[1] has made the infinite movement of resignation and can do no more, he will retain possession of Isaac only in his sorrow.

But what did Abraham? He arrived neither too early nor too late. He mounted his ass and rode slowly on his way. And all the while he had faith, believing that God would not demand Isaac of him, though ready all the while to sacrifice him, should it be demanded of him. He believed this on the strength of the absurd; for there was no question of human calculation any longer. And the absurdity consisted in God's, who yet made this demand of him, recalling his demand the very next moment. Abraham ascended the mountain and whilst the knife already gleamed in his hand he believed—that God would not demand Isaac of him. He was, to be sure, surprised at the outcome; but by a double movement he had returned at his first state of mind and therefore received Isaac back more gladly than the first time. . . .

On this height, then, stands Abraham. The last stage he loses sight of is that of infinite resignation. He does really proceed further, he arrives at faith. For all these caricatures of faith, wretched lukewarm sloth, which thinks. "Oh, there is no hurry, it is not necessary to worry before the time comes"; and miserable hopefulness, which says: "One

---

[1] By his own impulse and on his own responsibility.

cannot know what will happen, there might perhaps," all these caricatures belong to the sordid view of life and have already fallen under the infinite scorn of infinite resignation.

Abraham, I am not able to understand; and in a certain sense I can learn nothing from him without being struck with wonder. They who flatter themselves that by merely considering the outcome of Abraham's story they will necessarily arrive at faith, only deceive themselves and wish to cheat God out of the first movement of faith—it were tantamount to deriving worldly wisdom from the paradox. But who knows, one or the other of them may succeed in doing this; for our times are not satisfied with faith, and not even with the miracle of changing water into wine—they "go right on" changing wine into water.

Is it not preferable to remain satisfied with faith, and is it not outrageous that every one wishes to "go right on". If people in our times decline to be satisfied with love, as is proclaimed from various sides, where will we finally land? In worldly shrewdness, in mean calculation, in paltriness and baseness, in all that which renders man's divine origin doubtful. Were it not better to stand fast in the faith, and better that he that standeth take heed lest he fall;[1] for the movement of faith must ever be made by virtue of the absurd, but, note well, in such wise that one does not lose the things of this world but wholly and entirely regains them.

As far as I am concerned, I am able to describe most excellently the movements of faith; but I cannot make them myself. When a person wishes to learn how to swim he has himself suspended in a swimming-belt and then goes through the motions; but that does not mean that he can swim. In the same fashion I too can go through the motions of faith; but when I am thrown into the water I swim, to be sure (for I am not a wader in the shallows), but I go through a different set of movements, to-wit, those of infinity; whereas faith does the opposite, to-wit, makes the movements to regain the finite after having made those of infinite resignation. Blessed is he who can make these movements, for he performs a marvellous feat, and I shall never weary of admiring him, whether now it be Abraham himself or the slave in Abraham's house, whether it be a professor of philosophy or a poor servant-girl: it is all the same to me, for I have regard only to the movements. But these movements I watch closely, and I will not be

---

[1] Cf. I Cor. 10,12.

deceived, whether by myself or by anyone else. The knights of infinite resignation are easily recognized, for their gait is dancing and bold. But they who possess the jewel of faith frequently deceive one because their bearing is curiously like that of a class of people heartily despised by infinite resignation as well as by faith—the philistines.

Let me admit frankly that I have not in my experience encountered any certain specimen of this type; but I do not refuse to admit that as far as I know, every other person may be such a specimen. At the same time I will say that I have searched vainly for years. It is the custom of scientists to travel around the globe to see rivers and mountains, new stars, gay-colored birds, misshapen fish, ridiculous races of men. They abandon themselves to a bovine stupor which gapes at existence and believe they have seen something worthwhile. All this does not interest me; but if I knew where there lived such a knight of faith I would journey to him on foot, for that marvel occupies my thoughts exclusively. Not a moment would I leave him out of sight, but would watch how he makes the movements, and I would consider myself provided for life, and would divide my time between watching him and myself practicing the movements, and would thus use all my time in admiring him,

As I said, I have not met with such a one; but I can easily imagine him. Here he is. I make his acquaintance and am introduced to him. The first moment I lay my eyes on him I push him back, leaping back myself, I hold up my hands in amazement and say to myself: "Good Lord! that person? Is it really he—why, he looks like a parish-beadle!" But it is really he. I become more closely acquainted with him, watching his every movement to see whether some trifling incongruous movement of his has escaped me, some trace, perchance, of a signaling from the infinite, a glance, a look, a gesture, a melancholy air, or a smile, which might betray the presence of infinite resignation contrasting with the finite.

But no! I examine his figure from top to toe to discover whether there be anywhere a chink through which the infinite might be seen to peer forth. But no! he is of a piece, all through. And how about his footing? Vigorous, altogether that of finiteness, no citizen dressed in his very best, prepared to spend his Sunday afternoon in the park, treads the ground more firmly. He belongs altogether to this world, no philistine more so. There is no trace of the somewhat exclusive and haughty demeanor which marks off the knight of infinite resignation. He takes pleasure in all, things, is interested in everything, and perseveres in whatever he does with the zest characteristic of persons wholly given to worldly things. He attends to his business, and when one sees him one might think he was a clerk who had lost his soul in doing double bookkeeping, he is so exact. He takes a day off on Sundays. He goes to church. But no hint of anything supernatural or any other sign of the incommensurable betrays him, and if one did not know him it would be impossible to distinguish him in the congregation, for his brisk and manly singing proves only that he has a pair of good lungs.

In the afternoon he walks out to the forest. He takes delight in all he sees, in the crowds of men and women, the new omnibuses, the Sound—if one met him on the promenade one might think he was some shopkeeper who was having a good time, so simple is his joy; for he is not a poet, and in vain have I tried to lure him into betraying some sign of the poet's detachment. Toward evening he walks home again, with a gait as steady as that of a mail-carrier. On his way he happens to wonder whether his wife will have some little special warm dish ready for him, when he comes home—as she surely has—as, for instance, a roasted lamb's head garnished with greens. And if he met one minded like him he is very likely to continue talking about this dish with him till they reach the East Gate, and to talk about it with a zest befitting a chef. As it happens, he has not four shillings to spare, and yet he firmly believes that his wife surely has that dish ready for him. If she has, it would be an enviable sight for distinguished people, and an inspiring one for common folks, to see him eat, for he has an appetite greater than Esau's. His wife has not prepared it—strange, he remains altogether the same.

Again, on his way he passes a building lot and there meets another man. They fall to talking, and in a trice he erects a building, freely disposing of everything necessary. And the stranger will leave him with the impression that he has been talking with a capitalist—the fact being that the knight of my admiration is busy with the thought that if it really came to the point he would unquestionably have the means wherewithal at his disposal.

Now he is lying on his elbows in the window and looking over the square on which he lives. All that happens there, if it be only a rat creeping into a gutter-hole, or children playing together—everything engages his attention, and yet his mind is at rest as though it were the mind of a girl of sixteen. He smokes his pipe in the evening, and to look at him you would swear it was the green-grocer from across the street who is lounging at the window in the evening twilight. Thus he shows as much unconcern as any worthless happy-go-lucky fellow;

and yet, every moment he lives he purchases his leisure at the highest price, for he makes not the least movement except by virtue of the absurd; and yet, yet—indeed, I might become furious with anger, if for no other reason than that of envy—and yet, this man has performed, and is performing every moment, the movement of infinity . . . He has resigned everything absolutely, and then again seized hold of it all on the strength of the absurd. . .

But this miracle may so easily deceive one that it will be best if I describe the movements in a given case which may illustrate their aspect in contact with reality; and that is the important point. Suppose, then, a young swain falls in love with a princess, and all his life is bound up in this love. But circumstances are such that it is out of the question to think of marrying her, an impossibility to translate his dreams into reality. The slaves of paltriness, the frogs in the sloughs of life, they will shout, of course: "Such a love is folly, the rich brewer's widow is quite as good and solid a match." Let them but croak. The knight of infinite resignation does not follow their advice, he does not surrender his love, not for all the riches in the world. He is no fool, he first makes sure that this love really is the contents of his life, for his soul is too sound and too proud to waste itself on a mere intoxication. He is no coward, he is not afraid to let his love insinuate itself into his most secret and most remote thoughts, to let it wind itself in innumerable coils about every fiber of his consciousness—if he is disappointed in his love he will never be able to extricate himself again. He feels a delicious pleasure in letting love thrill his every nerve, and yet his soul is solemn as is that of him who has drained a cup of poison and who now feels the virus mingle with every drop of his blood, poised in that moment between life and death.

Having thus imbibed love, and being wholly absorbed in it, he does not lack the courage to try and dare all. He surveys the whole situation, he calls together his swift thoughts which like tame pigeons obey his every beck, he gives the signal, and they dart in all directions. But when they return, every one bearing a message of sorrow, and explain to him that it is impossible, then he becomes silent, he dismisses them, he remains alone; and then he makes the movement. Now if what I say here is to have any significance, it is of prime importance that the movement be made in a normal fashion. The knight of resignation is supposed to have sufficient energy to concentrate the entire contents of his life and the realization of existing conditions into one single wish. But if one lacks this concentration, this devotion to a single thought; if his soul from the very beginning is scattered on a number of objects, he will never be able to make the movement—he will be as worldly-wise in the conduct of his life as the financier who invests his capital in a number of securities to win on the one if he should lose on the other; that is, he is no knight. Furthermore, the knight is supposed to possess sufficient energy to concentrate all his thought into a single act of consciousness. If he lacks this concentration he will only run errands in life and will never be able to assume the attitude of infinite resignation; for the very minute he approaches it he will suddenly discover that he forgot something so that he must remain behind. The next minute, thinks he, it will be attainable again, and so it is; but such inhibitions will never allow him to make the movement but will, rather, tend to him sink ever deeper into the mire.

Our knight, then, performs the movement—which movement? Is he intent on forgetting the whole affair, which, too, would presuppose much concentration? No, for the knight does not contradict himself, and it is a contradiction to forget the main contents of one's life and still remain the same person. And he has no desire to become another person; neither does he consider such a desire to smack of greatness. Only lower natures forget themselves and become something different. Thus the butterfly has forgotten that it once was a caterpillar—who knows but it may forget her that it once was a butterfly, and turn into a fish! Deeper natures never forget themselves and never change their essential qualities. So the knight remembers all; but precisely this remembrance is painful. Nevertheless, in his infinite resignation he has become reconciled with existence. His love for the princess has become for him the expression of an eternal love, has assumed a religious character, has been transfigured into a love for the eternal being which, to be sure, denied him the fulfillment of his love, yet reconciled him again by presenting him with the abiding consciousness of his love's being preserved in an everlasting form of which no reality can rob him. . . .

Now, he is no longer interested in what the princess may do, and precisely this proves that he has made the movement of infinite resignation correctly. In fact, this is a good criterion for detecting whether a person's movement is sincere or just make-believe. Take a person who believes that he too has resigned, but lo! time passed, the princess did something on her part, for example, married a prince, and then his soul lost the elasticity of its resignation. This ought to show him that he did not make the movement correctly, for he who has resigned absolutely is sufficient unto himself. The knight does not cancel his resignation, but preserves his love as fresh and young as it was at the first moment, he never lets go of it just because his resignation is absolute. Whatever the princess does, cannot disturb him, for it is only the lower natures who have the law for their actions in some other person, i.e. have the premises of their actions outside of themselves. ...

Infinite resignation is the last stage which goes before faith, so that everyone who has not made the movement of infinite resignation cannot have faith; for only through absolute resignation do I become conscious of my eternal worth, and only then can there arise the problem of again grasping hold of this world by virtue of faith.

We will now suppose the knight of faith in the same case. He does precisely as the other knight, he absolutely resigns the love which is the contents of his life, he is reconciled to the pain; but then the miraculous happens, he makes one more movement, strange beyond comparison, saying: "And still I believe that I shall marry her—marry her by virtue of the absurd, by virtue of the act that to God nothing is impossible." Now the absurd is not one of the categories which belong to the understanding proper. It is not identical with the improbable, the unforeseen, the unexpected. The very moment our knight resigned himself he made sure of the absolute impossibility, in any human sense, of his love. This was the result reached by his reflections, and he had sufficient energy to make them. In a transcendent sense, however, by his very resignation, the attainment of his end is not impossible; but this very act of again taking possession of his love is at the same time a relinquishment of it. Nevertheless this kind of possession is by no means an absurdity to the intellect; for the intellect all the while continues to be right, as it is aware that in the world of finalities, in which reason rules, his love was and is, an impossibility. The knight of faith realizes this fully as well. Hence the only thing which can save him is recourse to the absurd, and this recourse he has through his faith. That is, he clearly recognizes the impossibility, and in the same moment he believes the absurd; for if he imagined he had faith, without at the same time recognizing, with all the passion his soul is capable of, that his love is impossible, he would be merely deceiving himself, and his testimony would be of no value, since he had not arrived even at the stage of absolute resignation. ...

This last movement, the paradoxical movement of faith, I cannot make, whether or no it be my duty, although I desire nothing more ardently than to be able to make it. It must be left to a person's discretion whether he cares to make this confession; and at any rate, it is a matter between him and the Eternal Being, who is the object of his faith, whether an amicable adjustment can be affected. But what every person can do is to make the movement of absolute resignation, and I for my part would not hesitate to declare him a coward who imagines he cannot perform it. It is a different matter with faith. But what no person has a right to, is to delude others into the belief that faith is something of no great significance, or that it is an easy matter, whereas it is the greatest and most difficult of all things.

But the story of Abraham is generally interpreted in a different way. God's mercy is praised which restored Isaac to him—it was but a trial! A trial. This word may mean much or little, and yet the whole of it passes off as quickly as the story is told: one mounts a winged horse, in the same instant one arrives on Mount Moriah, and presto one sees the ram. It is not remembered that Abraham only rode on an ass which travels but slowly, that it was a three days' journey for him, and that he required some additional time to collect the firewood, to bind Isaac, and to whet his knife.

And yet one extols Abraham. He who is to preach the sermon may sleep comfortably until a quarter of an hour before he is to preach it, and the listener may comfortably sleep during the sermon, for everything is made easy enough, without much exertion either to preacher or listener. But now suppose a man was present who suffered with sleeplessness and who went home and sat in a corner and reflected as follows: "The whole lasted but a minute, you need only wait a little while, and then the ram will be shown and the trial will be over." Now if the preacher should find him in this frame of mind, I believe he would confront him in all his dignity and say to him: "Wretch that thou art, to let thy soul lapse into such folly; miracles do not happen, all life is a trial." And as he proceeded he would grow more and more passionate, and would become ever more satisfied with himself; and whereas he had not noticed any congestion in his head whilst preaching about Abraham, he now feels the veins on his forehead swell. Yet who knows but he would stand aghast if the sinner should answer him in a quiet and dignified manner that it was precisely this about which he preached the Sunday before.

Let us then either waive the whole story of Abraham, or else learn to stand in awe of the enormous paradox which constitutes his significance for us, so that we may learn to understand that our age, like every age, may rejoice if it has faith. If the story of Abraham is not a mere nothing, an illusion, or if it is just used for show and as a pastime, the mistake cannot by any means be in the sinner's wishing to do likewise; but it is necessary to find out how great was the deed which Abraham performed, in order that the man may judge for himself whether he has the courage and the mission to do likewise. The comical contradiction in the procedure of the preacher was his reduction of the story of Abraham to insignificance whereas he rebuked the other man for doing the very same thing.

But should we then cease to speak about Abraham? I certainly think not. But if I were to speak about him I would first of all describe the terrors of his trial. To that end leechlike I would suck all the suffering and distress out of the anguish of a father, in order to be able to describe what Abraham suffered whilst yet preserving his faith. I would remind the hearer that the journey lasted three days and a goodly part of the fourth—in fact, these three and half days ought to become infinitely longer than the few thousand years which separate me from Abraham. I would remind him, as I think right, that every person is still permitted to turn about before trying his strength on this formidable task; in fact, that he may return every instant in repentance. Provided this is done, I fear for nothing. Nor do I fear to awaken great desire among people to attempt to emulate Abraham. But to get out a cheap edition of Abraham and yet forbid every one to do as he did, that I call ridiculous.[1]

---

[1] The above, with the omissions indicated, constitutes about one-third of "Fear and Trembling."

Preparation for a Christian Life

Part I[1]

"COME HITHER UNTO ME,
ALL YE THAT LABOR AND ARE HEAVY LADEN,
AND I WILL GIVE YOU REST."
(MATTHEW 11,28.)
THE INVITATION

I

"C o m e h i t h e r!"—It is not at all strange if he who is in danger and needs help—speedy, immediate help, perhaps—it is not strange if he cries out: "come hither"! Nor it is strange that a quack cries his wares: "come hither, I cure all maladies"; alas, for in the case of the quack it is only too true that it is the physician who has need of the sick. "Come hither all ye who at extortionate prices can pay for the cure—or at any rate for the medicine; here is physic for everybody—who can pay; come hither!"

In all other cases, however, it is generally true that he who can help must be sought; and, when found, may be difficult of access; and, if access is had, his help may have to be implored a long time; and when his help has been implored a long time, he may be moved only with difficulty, that is, he sets a high price on his services; and sometimes, precisely when he refuses payment or generously asks for none, it is only an expression of how infinitely high he values his services. On the other hand, he[2] who sacrificed himself, he sacrifices himself, here

---

[1] First Part; comprising about one-fourth of the whole book.
[2] I. e. Christ; cf. Introduction p. 41 for the use of small letters.

too; it is indeed he who seeks those in need of help, is himself the one who goes about and calls, almost imploringly: "come hither!" He, the only one who can help, and help with what alone is indispensable, and can save from the one truly mortal disease, he does not wait for people to come to him, but comes himself, without having been called; for it is he who calls out to them, it is he who holds out help—and what help! Indeed, that simple sage of antiquity[1] was as infinitely right as the majority who do the opposite are wrong, in setting no great price, whether on himself or his instruction; even if he thus in a certain sense proudly expressed the utter difference in kind between payment and his services. But he was not so solicitous as to beg anyone to come to him, notwithstanding—or shall I say because?—he was not altogether sure what his help signified; for the more sure one is that his help is the only one obtainable, the more reason has he, in a human sense, to ask a great price for it; and the less sure one is, the more reason has he to offer freely the possible help he has, in order to do at least something for others. But he who calls himself the Savior, and knows that he is, he calls out solicitously: "come hither unto me!"

"Come hither a l l y e!"—Strange! For if he who, when it comes to the point, perhaps cannot help a single one—if such a one should boastfully invite everybody, that would not seem so very strange, man's nature being such as it is. But if a man is absolutely sure of being able to help, and at the same time willing to help, willing to devote his all in doing so, and with all sacrifices, then he generally makes at least one reservation; which is, to make a choice among those he means to help. That is, however willing one may be, still it is not everybody one cares to help; one does not care to sacrifice one's self to that extent. But he, the only one who can really help, and really help everybody—the only one, therefore, who really can invite everybody—he makes no conditions whatever; but utters the invitation which, from the beginning of the world, seems to have been reserved for him: "Come hither all ye!" Ah, human self--sacrifice, even when thou art most beautiful and noble, when we admire thee most: this is a sacrifice still greater, which is, to sacrifice every provision for one's own self, so that in one's willingness to help there is not even the least partiality. Ah, the love that sets no price on one's self, that makes one forget altogether that he is the helper, and makes one altogether blind as to who it is one helps, but infinitely careful only that he be a suffer-

---

[1] Socrates.

er, whatever else he may be; and thus willing unconditionally to help everybody—different, alas! in this from everybody!

"Come hither u n t o m e!" Strange! For human compassion also, and willingly, does something for them that labor and are heavy laden; one feeds the hungry, clothes the naked, makes charitable gifts, builds charitable institutions, and if the compassion be heartfelt, perhaps even visits those that labor and are heavy laden. But to invite them to come to one, that will never do, because then all one's household and manner of living would have to be changed. For a man cannot himself live in abundance, or at any rate in well-being and happiness, and at the same time dwell in one and the same house together with, and in daily intercourse with, the poor and miserable, with them that labor and are heavy laden! In order to be able to invite them in such wise, a man must himself live altogether in the same way, as poor as the poorest, as lowly as the lowliest, familiar with the sorrows and sufferings of life, and altogether belonging to the same station as they, whom he invites, that is, they who labor and are heavy laden. If he wishes to invite a sufferer, he must either change his own condition to be like that of the sufferer, or else change that of the sufferer to be like his own; for if this is not done the difference will stand out only the more by contrast. And if you wish to invite all those who suffer—for you may make an exception with one of them and change his condition—it can be done only in one way, which is, to change your condition so as to live as they do; provided your life be not already lived thus, as was the case with him who said: "Come hither unto me, all ye that labor and are heavy laden!" Thus said he; and they who lived with him saw him, and behold! there was not even the least thing in his manner of life to contradict it. With the silent and truthful eloquence of actual performance his life expresses—even though he had never in his life said these words—his life expresses: "Come hither unto me, all ye that labor and are heavy laden"! He abides by his word, or he him-self is the word; he is what he says, and also in this sense he is the Word.[1]

"A l l y e t h a t l a b o r a n d a r e h e a v y l a d e n." Strange! His only concern is lest there be a single one who labors and is heavy laden who does not hear this invitation. Neither does he fear that too many will come. Ah, heart-room makes house-room; but where wilt thou find heart-room, if not in his heart? He leaves it to each one how

---

[1] John I,1.

to understand his invitation: he has a clear conscience about it, for he has invited all those that labor and are heavy laden.

But what means it, then, to labor and be heavy laden? Why does he not offer a clearer explanation so that one may know exactly whom he means, and why is he so chary of his words? Ah, thou narrow-minded one, he is so chary of his words, lest he be narrow-minded; and thou narrow-hearted one, he is so chary of his words lest he be narrow-hearted. For such is his love—and love has regard to all—as to prevent anyone from troubling and searching his heart whether he too be among those invited. And he who would insist on a more definite explanation, is he not likely to be some self-loving person who is calculating whether this explanation does not particularly fit himself; one who does not consider that the more of such exact explanations are offered, the more certainly some few would be left in doubt as to whether they were invited? Ah man, why does thine eye see only thyself, why is it evil because he is good?[1] The invitation to all men opens the arms of him who invites, and thus he stands of aspect everlasting; but no sooner is a closer explanation attempted which might help one or the other to another kind of certainty, than his aspect would be transformed and, as it were, a shadow of change would pass over his countenance.

"I w i l l g i v e y o u r e s t." Strange! For then the words "come hither unto me" must be understood to mean: stay with me, I am rest; or, it is rest to remain with me. It is not, then, as in other cases where he who helps and says "come hither" must afterwards say: "now depart again," explaining to each one where the help he needs is to be found, where the healing herb grows which will cure him, or where the quiet spot is found where he may rest from labor, or where the happier continent exists where one is not heavy laden. But no, he who opens his arms, inviting every one—ah, if all, all they that labor and are heavy laden came to him, he would fold them all to his heart, saying: "stay with me now; for to stay with me is rest." The helper himself is the help. Ah, strange, he who invites everybody and wishes to help everybody, his manner of treating the sick is as if calculated for every sick man, and as if every sick man who comes to him were his only patient. For otherwise a physician divides his time among many patients who, however great their number, still are far, far from being all mankind. He will prescribe the medicine, he will say what is to be done, and

---

[1] Matthew 20,15.

how it is to be used, and then he will go—to some other patient; or, in case the patient should visit him, he will let him depart. The physician cannot remain sitting all day with one patient, and still less can he have all his patients about him in his home, and yet sit all day with one patient without neglecting the others. For this reason the helper and his help are not one and the same thing. The help which the physician prescribes is kept with him by the patient all day so that he may constantly use it, whilst the physician visits him now and again; or he visits the physician now and again. But if the helper is also the help, why, then he will stay with the sick man all day, or the sick man with him—ah, strange that it is just this helper who invites all men!

II

COME HITHER ALL YE THAT LABOR AND ARE HEAVY LADEN, I WILL GIVE YOU REST.

What enormous multiplicity, what an almost boundless adversity, of people invited; for a man, a lowly man, may, indeed, try to enumerate only a few of these diversities—that he who invites must invite all men, even if every one especially and individually.

The invitation goes forth, then—along the highways and byways, and along the loneliest paths; aye, goes forth ere there is a path so lonely that one man only, and no one else, knows of it, and goes forth where there is but one track, the track of the wretched one who fled along that path with his misery, that and no other track; goes forth even where there is no path to show how one may return: even where the invitation penetrates and by itself easily and surely finds its way back—most easily, indeed, when it brings the fugitive along to him that issued the invitation. Come hither, come hither all ye, also thou, and thou, and thou, too, thou loneliest of all fugitives!

Thus the invitation goes forth and remains standing, wheresoever there is a parting of the ways, in order to call out. Ah, just as the trumpet call of the soldiers is directed to the four quarters of the globe, likewise does this invitation sound wherever there is a meeting of roads; with no uncertain sound—for who would then come?—but with the certitude of eternity.

It stands by the parting of the ways where worldly and earthly sufferings have set down their crosses, and calls out: Come hither, all ye poor and wretched ones, ye who in poverty must slave in order to as-

Søren Kierkegaard

sure yourselves, not of a care-free, but of a toilsome, future; ah, bitter contradiction, to have to slave for—a s s u r i n g one's self of that under which one groans, of that which one f l e e s! Ye despised and overlooked ones, about whose existence no one, aye, no one is concerned, not so much even as about some domestic animal which is of greater value! Ye sick, and halt, and blind, and deaf, and crippled, come hither!—Ye bed-ridden, aye, come hither, ye too; for the invitation makes bold to invite even the bed-ridden—to come! Ye lepers; for the invitation breaks down all differences in order to unite all, it wishes to make good the hardship caused by the difference in men, the difference which seats one as a ruler over millions, in possession of all gifts of fortune, and drives another one out into the wilderness—and why? (ah, the cruelty of it!) because (ah, the cruel human inference!) b e c a u s e he is wretched, indescribably wretched. Why then? Because he stands in need of help, or at any rate, of compassion. And why, then? Because human compassion is a wretched thing which is cruel when there is the greatest need of being compassionate, and compassionate only when, at bottom, it is not true compassion! Ye sick of heart, Ye who only through your anguish learned to know that a man's heart and an animal's heart are two different things, and what it means to be sick at heart—what it means when the physician may be right in declaring one sound of heart and yet heart-sick; ye whom faithlessness deceived and whom human sympathy—for the sympathy of man is rarely late in coming—whom human sympathy made a target for mockery; all ye wronged and aggrieved and ill-used; all ye noble ones who, as any and everybody will be able to tell you, deservedly reap the reward of ingratitude (for why were ye simple enough to be noble, why foolish enough to be kindly, and disinterested, and faithful)—all ye victims of cunning, of deceit, of backbiting, of envy, whom baseness chose as its victim and cowardice left in the lurch, whether now ye be sacrificed in remote and lonely places, after having crept away in order to die, or whether ye be trampled underfoot in the thronging crowds where no one asks what rights ye have, and no one, what wrongs ye suffer, and no one, where ye smart or how ye smart, whilst the crowd with brute force tramples you into the dust—come ye hither!

The invitation stands at the parting of the ways, where death parts death and life. Come hither all ye that sorrow and ye that vainly labor! For indeed there is rest in the grave; but to sit by a grave, or to stand by a grave, or to visit a grave, all that is far from lying in the grave;

and to read to one's self again and again one's own words which he knows by heart, the epitaph which one devised one's self and understands best, namely, who it is that lies buried h e r e, all that is not the same as to lie buried one's self. In the grave there is rest, but by the grave there is no rest; for it is said: so far and no farther, and so you may as well go home again. But however often, whether in your thoughts or in fact, you return to t h a t grave—you will never get any farther, you will not get away from the spot, and this is very trying and is by no means rest. Come ye hither, therefore: here is the way by which one may go farther, here is rest by the grave, rest from the sorrow over loss, or rest in the sorrow of loss—through him who everlastingly re‐unites those that are parted, and more firmly than nature unites parents with their children, and children with their parents—for, alas! they were parted; and more closely than the minister unites husband and wife—for, alas! their separation did come to pass; and more indissolubly than the bond of friendship unites friend with friend—for, alas! it was broken. Separation penetrated everywhere and brought with it sorrow and unrest; but here is rest!—Come hither also ye who had your abodes assigned you among the graves, ye who are considered dead to human society, but neither missed nor mourned—not buried and yet dead; that is, belonging neither to life nor to death; ye, alas! to whom human society cruelly closed its doors and for whom no grave has as yet opened itself in pity—come hither, ye also, here is rest, and here is life!

The invitation stands at the parting of the ways, where the road of sin turns away from the enclosure of innocence—ah, come hither, ye are so close to him; but a single step in the opposite direction, and ye are infinitely far from him. Very possibly ye do not yet stand in need of rest, nor grasp fully what that means; but still follow the invitation, so that he who invites may save you from a predicament out of which it is so difficult and dangerous to be saved; and so that, being saved, ye may stay with him who is the Savior of all, likewise of innocence. For even if it were possible that innocence be found somewhere, and altogether pure: why should not innocence also need a savior to keep it safe from evil?—The invitation stands at the parting of the ways, where the road of sin turns away, to enter more deeply into sin. Come hither all ye who have strayed and have been lost, whatever may have been your error and sin: whether one more pardonable in the sight of man and nevertheless perhaps more frightful, or one more terrible in the sight of man and yet, perchance, more pardonable; whether it be one which became known here on earth or one which, though hidden, yet is known in heaven—and even if ye found pardon here on earth without finding rest in your souls, or found no pardon because ye did not seek it, or because ye sought it in vain: ah, return and come hither, here is rest!

The invitation stands at the parting of the ways, where the road of sin turns away for the last time and to the eye is lost in perdition. Ah, return, return, and come hither! Do not shrink from the difficulties of the retreat, however great; do not fear the irksome way of conversion, however laboriously it may lead to salvation; whereas sin with winged speed and growing pace leads forward or—downward, so easily, so indescribably easy—as easily, in fact, as when a horse, altogether freed from having to pull, cannot even with all his might stop the vehicle which pushes him into the abyss. Do not despair over each relapse which the God of patience has patience enough to pardon, and which a sinner should surely have patience enough to humble himself under. Nay, fear nothing and despair not: he that sayeth "come hither," he is with you on the way, from him come help and pardon on that way of conversion which leads to him; and with him is rest.

Come hither all, all ye—with him is rest; and he will raise no difficulties, he does but one thing: he opens his arms. He will not first ask you, you sufferer—as righteous men, alas, are accustomed to, even when willing to help—"Are you not perhaps yourself the cause of your misfortune, have you nothing with which to reproach yourself?" It is so easy to fall into this very human error, and from appearances to judge a man's success or failure: for instance, if a man is a cripple, or deformed, or has an unprepossessing appearance, to infer that therefore he is a bad man; or, when a man is unfortunate enough to suffer reverses so as to be ruined or so as to go down in the world, to infer that therefore he is a vicious man. Ah, and this is such an exquisitely cruel pleasure, this being conscious of one's own righteousness as against the sufferer—explaining his afflictions as God's punishment, so that one does not even—dare to help him; or asking him that question which condemns him and flatters our own righteousness, before helping him. But he will not ask you thus, will not in such cruel fashion be your benefactor. And if you are yourself conscious of your sin he will not ask about it, will not break still further the bent reed, but raise you up, if you will but join him. He will not point you out by way of contrast, and place you outside of himself, so that your sin will stand out as still more terrible, but he will grant you a hiding place within him; and hidden within him your sins will be hidden. For he is the friend of sinners. Let him but behold a sinner, and he not only stands still, opening his arms and saying "come hither," nay, but he stands—and waits, as did the father of the prodigal son; or he does not merely remain standing and waiting, but goes out to search, as the shepherd went forth to search for the strayed sheep, or as the woman went to search for the lost piece of silver. He goes—nay, he has gone, but an infinitely longer way than any shepherd or any woman, for did he not go the infinitely long way from being God to becoming man, which he did to seek sinners?

III

COME HITHER UNTO ME
ALL YE THAT LABOR AND ARE HEAVYLADEN,
AND I WILL GIVE YOU REST.

"C o m e h i t h e r!" For he supposes that they that labor and are heavy laden feel their burden and their labor, and that they stand there now, perplexed and sighing—one casting about with his eyes to discover whether there is help in sight anywhere; another with his eyes fixed on the ground, because he can see no consolation; and a third with his eyes staring heavenward, as though help was bound to come from heaven—but all seeking. Therefore he sayeth: "come hither!" But he invites not him who has ceased to seek and to sorrow. -"C o m e h i t h e r!" For he who invites knows that it is a mark of true suffering, if one walks alone and broods in silent disconsolateness, without courage to confide in any one, and with even less self-confidence to dare to hope for help. Alas, not only he whom we read about was possessed of a dumb devil.[1] No suffering which does not first of all render the sufferer dumb is of much significance, no more than the love which does not render one silent; for those sufferers who run on about their afflictions neither labor nor are heavy laden. Behold, therefore the inviter will not wait till they that labor and are heavy laden come to him, but calls them lovingly; for all his willingness to help might, perhaps, be of no avail if he did not say these words and thereby take the first step; for in the call of these words: "come hither unto me!" he comes himself to them. Ah, human compassion—sometimes, perhaps, it is indeed praiseworthy self-restraint, sometimes, perhaps, even true compassion, which may cause you to refrain from questioning him whom you

---

[1] Luke 11, 14.

suppose to be brooding over a hidden affliction; but also, how often indeed is this compassion but worldly wisdom which does not care to know too much! Ah, human compassion—how often was it not pure curiosity, and not compassion, which prompted you to venture into the secret of one afflicted; and how burdensome it was—almost like a punishment of your curiosity—when he accepted your invitation and came to you! But he who sayeth these redeeming words "Come hither!" he is not deceiving himself in saying these words, nor will he deceive you when you come to him in order to find rest by throwing your burden on him. He follows the promptings of his heart in saying these words, and his heart follows his words; if you then follow these words, they will follow you back again to his heart. This follows as a matter of course—ah, will you not follow the invitation?—"C o m e h i t h e r!" For supposes that they that labor and are heavy laden are so worn out and overtaxed, and so near swooning that they have forgotten, as though in a stupor, that there is such thing as consolation. Alas, or he knows for sure that there is no consolation and no help unless it is sought from him; and therefore must he call out to them "Come hither!"

"C o m e h i t h e r!" For is it not so that every society has some symbol or token which is worn by those who belong to it? When a young girl is adorned in a certain manner one knows that she is going to the dance: Come hither all ye that labor and are heavy laden—come hither! You need not carry an external and visible badge; come but with A- your head anointed and your face washed, if only you labor in your heart and are heavy laden.

"Come hither!" Ah, do not stand still and consider; nay, consider, consider that with every moment you stand still after having heard the invitation you will hear the call more faintly and thus withdraw from it, even though you are standing still.—"Come hither!" Ah, however weary and faint you be from work, or from the long, long and yet hitherto fruitless search for help and salvation, and even though you may feel as if you could not take one more step, and not wait one more moment, without dropping to the ground: ah, but this one step and here is rest!—"Come hither!" But if, alas, there be one who is so wretched that he cannot come?—Ah, a sigh is sufficient; your mere sighing for him is also to come hither.

THE PAUSE

COME HITHER UNTO ME ALL YE THAT LABOR AND ARE HEAVY LADEN, AND I SHALL GIVE YOU REST.

Pause now! But what is there to give pause? That which in the same instant makes all undergo an absolute change—so that, instead of seeing an immense throng of them that labor and are heavy laden following the invitation, you will in the end behold the very opposite, that is, an immense throng of men who flee back shudderingly, scrambling to get away, trampling all down before them; so that, if one were to infer the sense of what had been said from the result it produced, one would have to infer that the words had been "procul o procul este profani", rather than "come hither"—that gives pause which is infinitely more important and infinitely more decisive: THE PERSON OF HIM WHO INVITES. Not in the sense that he is not the man to do what he has said, or not God, to keep what he has promised; no, in a very different sense.

Pause is given by the fact that he who invites is, and insists on being, the definite historic person he was 1800 years ago, and that he as this definite person, and living under the conditions then obtaining, spoke these words of invitation.—He is not, and does not wish to be, one about whom one may simply know something from history (i.e. world history, history proper, as against Sacred History) ; for from history one cannot "learn" anything about him, the simple reason being that nothing can be "known" about him.—He does not wish to be judged in a human way, from the results of his life; that is, he is and wishes to be, a rock of offense and the object of faith. To judge him after the consequences of his life is a blasphemy, for being God, his life, and the very fact that he was then living and really did live, is infinitely more important than all the consequences of it in history.

a. Who spoke these words of invitation?

He that invites. Who is he? Jesus Christ. Which Jesus Christ? He that sits in glory on the right side of his Father? No. From his seat of glory he spoke not a single word. Therefore it is Jesus Christ in his lowliness, and in the condition of lowliness, who spoke these words.

Is then Jesus Christ not the same? Yes, verily, he is today, and was yesterday, and 1800 years ago, the same who abased himself, assuming the form of a servant—the Jesus Christ who spake these words of invitation. It is also he who hath said that he would return again in glory. In his return in glory he is, again, the same Jesus Christ; but this has not yet come to pass.

Is he then not in glory now? Assuredly, that the Christian b e l i e v e s. But it was in his lowly condition that he spoke these words; he did not speak them from his glory. And about his return in glory nothing can be known, for this can in the strictest sense be a matter of belief only. But a believer one cannot become except by having gone to him in his lowly condition—to him, the rock of offense and the object of faith. In other shape he does not exist, for only thus did he exist. That he will return in glory is indeed expected, but can be expected and believed only by him who believes, and has believed, in him as he was here on earth.

Jesus Christ is, then, the same; yet lived he 1800 years ago in debasement, and is transfigured only at his return. As yet he has not returned; therefore he is still the one in lowly guise about whom we believe that he will return in glory. Whatever he said and taught, every word he spoke, becomes eo ipso untrue if we give it the appearance of having been spoken by Christ in his glory. Nay, he is silent. It is the l o w l y Christ who speaks. The space of time between (i.e. between his debasement and his return in glory) which is at present about 1800 years, and will possibly become many times 1800—this space of time, or else what this space of time tries to make of Christ, the worldly information about him furnished by world history or church history, as to who Christ was, as to who it was who really spoke these words—all this does not concern us, is neither here nor there, but only serves to corrupt our conception of him, and thereby renders untrue these words of invitation.

It is untruthful of me to impute to a person words which he never used. But it is likewise untruthful, and the words he used likewise become untruthful, or it becomes untrue that he used them, if I assign to him a nature essentially unlike the one he had when he did use them. Essentially unlike; for an untruth concerning this or the other trifling circumstance will not make it untrue that "he" said them. And therefore, if it please God to walk on earth in such strict incognito as only one all-powerful can assume, in guise impenetrable to all men; if it please him—and why he does it, for what purpose, that he knows best himself; but whatever the reason and the purpose, it is certain that the incognito is of essential significance—I say, if it please God to walk on earth in the guise of a servant and, to judge from his appearance, exactly like any other man; if it please him to teach men in this guise—if, now, any one repeats his very words, but gives the saying the appearance that it was God that spoke these words: then it is untruthful; for it is untrue that he said these words.

b. Can one from history[1] learn to know anything about Christ?

No. And why not? Because one cannot "know" anything at all about "Christ"; for he is the paradox, the object of faith, and exists only for faith. But all historic information is communication of "knowledge." Therefore one cannot learn anything about Christ from history. For whether now one learn little or much about him, it will not represent what he was in reality. Hence one learns something else about him than what is strictly true, and therefore learns nothing about him, or gets to know something wrong about him; that is, one is deceived. History makes Christ look different from what he looked in truth, and thus one learns much from history about—Christ? No, not about Christ; because about him nothing can be "known," he can only be believed.

c. Can one prove from history that Christ was God?

Let me first ask another question: is any more absurd contradiction thinkable than wishing to PROVE (no matter, for the present, whether one wishes to do so from history, or from whatever else in the wide world one wishes to prove it) that a certain person is God? To maintain that a certain person is God—that is, professes to be God—is indeed a stumbling block in the purest sense. But what is the nature of a stumbling block? It is an assertion which is at variance with all (human) reason. Now think of proving that! But to prove something is to render it reasonable and real. Is it possible, then, to render reasonable and real what is at variance with all reason? Scarcely; unless one wishes to contradict one's self. One can prove only that it is at variance with all reason. The proofs for the divinity of Christ given in Scripture, such as the miracles and his resurrection from the grave exist, too, only for faith; that is, they are no "proofs," for they are not meant to prove that all this agrees with reason but, on the contrary, are meant to prove that it is at variance with reason and therefore a matter of faith.

---

[1] Kierkegaard's note: by history we mean here profane history world history, history as such, as against Sacred History.

First, then, let us take up the proofs from history. "Is it not 1800 years ago now that Christ lived, is not his name proclaimed and reverenced throughout the world, has not his teaching (Christianity) changed the aspect of the world, having victoriously affected all affairs: has then history not sufficiently, or more than sufficiently, made good its claim as to who he was, and that he was-God?" No, indeed, history has by no means sufficiently, or more than sufficiently, made good its claim, and in fact history cannot accomplish this in all eternity. However, as to the first part of the statement, it is true enough that his name is proclaimed throughout the world—as to whether it is reverenced, that I do not presume to decide. Also, it is true enough that Christianity has transformed the aspect of the world, having victoriously affected all affairs, so victoriously indeed, that everybody now claims to be a Christian.

But what does this prove? It proves, at most, that Jesus Christ was a great man, the greatest, perhaps, who ever lived. But that he was God—stop now, that conclusion shall with God's help fall to the ground.

Now, if one intends to introduce this conclusion by assuming that Jesus Christ was a man, and then considers the 1800 years of history (i.e. the consequences of his life), one may indeed conclude with a constantly rising superlative: he was great, greater, the greatest, extraordinarily and astonishingly the greatest man who ever lived. If one begins, on the other hand, with the assumption (of faith) that he was God, one has by so doing stricken out and cancelled the 1800 years as not making the slightest difference, one way or the other, because the certainty of faith is on infinitely higher plane. And one course or the other one must take; but we shall arrive at sensible conclusions only if we take the latter.

If one takes the former course one will find it impossible—unless by committing the logical error of passing over into different category—one will find it impossible in the conclusion suddenly to arrive at the new category "God"; that is, one cannot make the consequence, or consequences, of—a man's life suddenly prove at a certain point in the argument that this man was God. If such a procedure were correct one ought to be able to answer satisfactorily a question like this: what must the consequence be, how great the effects, how many centuries must elapse, in order to infer from the consequences of a man's life—for such was the assumption—that he was God; or whether it is really the case that in the year 300 Christ had not yet been entirely proved to be God, though certainly the most extraordinarily, astonishingly, greatest man who had ever lived, but that a few more centuries would be necessary to prove that he was God. In that case we would be obliged to infer that people the fourth century did not look upon Christ as God, and still less they who lived in the first century; whereas the certainty that he was God would grow with every century. Also, that in our century this certainty would be greater than it had ever been, a certainty in comparison with which the first centuries hardly so much as glimpsed his divinity. You may answer this question or not, it does not matter.

In general, is it at all possible by the consideration of the gradually unfolding consequences of something to arrive at conclusion different in quality from what we started with? Is it not sheer insanity (providing man is sane) to let one's judgment become so altogether confused as to land in the wrong category? And if one begins with such a mistake, then how will one be able, at any subsequent point, to infer from the consequences of something, that one has to deal with an altogether different, in fact, infinitely different, category? A foot-print certainly is the consequence of some creature having made it. Now I may mistake the track for that of, let us say, a bird; whereas by nearer inspection, and by following it for some distance, I may make sure that it was made by some other animal. Very good; but there was no infinite difference in quality between my first assumption and my later conclusion. But can I on further consideration and following the track still further, arrive at the conclusion: therefore it was a spirit—a spirit that leaves no tracks? Precisely the same holds true of the argument that from the consequences of a human life—for that was the assumption—we may infer that therefore it was God.

Is God then so like man, is there so little difference between the two that, while in possession of my right senses, I may begin with the assumption that Christ was human? And, for that matter, has not Christ himself affirmed that he was God? On the other hand, if God and man resemble each other so closely, and are related to each other to such a degree—that is, essentially belong to the same category of beings, then the conclusion "therefore he was God" is nevertheless just humbug, because if that is all there is to being God, then God does not exist at all. But if God does exist and, therefore, belongs to a category infinitely different from man, why, then neither I nor anyone else can start with the assumption that Christ was human and end with the conclusion that therefore he was God. Anyone with a bit of logical sense will easily recognize that the whole question about the consequences of Christ's life on earth is incommensurable with the decision that he is God. In fact, this decision is to be made on an altogether different plane: man must decide for himself whether he will believe Christ to be what he himself affirmed he was, that is, God, or whether he will not believe so.

What has been said—mind you, providing one will take the time to understand it—is sufficient to make a logical mind stop drawing any inferences from the consequences of Christ's life: that therefore he was God. But faith in its own right protests against every attempt to approach Jesus Christ by the help of historical information about the consequences of his life. Faith contends that this whole attempt is b l a s p h e m o u s. Faith contends that the only proof left unimpaired by unbelief when it did away with all the other proofs of the truth of Christianity, the proof which—indeed, this is complicated business—I say, which unbelief invented in order to prove the truth of Christianity—the proof about which so excessively much ado has been made in Christendom, the proof of 1800 years: as to this, faith contends that it is—b l a s p h e m y.

With regard to a man it is true that the consequences of his life are more important than his life. If one, then, in order to find out who Christ was, and in order to find out by some inference, considers the consequences of his life: why, then one changes him into a man by this very act—a man who, like other men, is to pass his examination in history, and history is in this case as mediocre an examiner as any half-baked teacher in Latin.

But strange! By the help of history, that is, by considering the consequences of his life, one wishes to arrive at the conclusion that therefore, therefore he was God; and faith makes the exactly opposite contention that he who even begins with this syllogism is guilty of blasphemy. Nor does the blasphemy consist in assuming hypothetically that Christ was a man. No, the blasphemy consists in the thought which lies at the bottom of the whole business, the thought without which one would never start it, and of whose validity one is fully and firmly assured that it will hold also with regard to Christ—the thought that the consequences of his life are more important than his life; in other words, that he is a man. The hypothesis is: let us assume that Christ was a man; but at the bottom of this hypothesis, which is not blasphemy as yet, there lies the assumption that, the consequences of a man's life being more important than his life, this will hold true also of Christ. Unless this is assumed one must admit that one's whole argument is absurd, must admit it before beginning—so why begin at all? But once it is assumed, and the argument is started, we have the blasphemy. And the more one becomes absorbed in the consequences of

Christ's life, with the aim of being able to make sure whether or no he was God, the more blasphemous is one's conduct; and it remains blasphemous so long as this consideration is persisted in.

Curious coincidence: one tries to make it appear that, providing one but thoroughly considers the consequences of Christ's life, this "therefore" will surely be arrived at—and faith condemns the very beginning of this attempt as blasphemy, and hence the continuance in it as a worse blasphemy.

"History," says faith, "has nothing to do with Christ." With regard to him we have only Sacred History (which is different in kind from general history), Sacred History which tells of his life and career when in debasement, and tells also that he affirmed himself to be God. He is the paradox which history never will be able to digest or convert into a general syllogism. He is in his debasement the same as he is in his exaltation—but the 1800 years, or let it be 18,000 years, have nothing whatsoever to do with this. The brilliant consequences in the history of the world which are sufficient, almost, to convince even a professor of history that he was God, these brilliant consequences surely do not represent his return in glory! Forsooth, in that case it were imagined rather meanly! The same thing over again: Christ is thought to be a man whose return in glory can be, and can become, nothing else than the consequences of his life in history—whereas Christ's return in glory is something absolutely different and a matter of faith. He abased himself and was swathed in rags—he will return in glory; but the brilliant consequences in history, especially when examined a little more closely, are too shabby a glory—at any rate a glory of an altogether incongruous nature, of which faith therefore never speaks, when speaking about his glory. History is a very respectable science indeed, only it must not become so conceited as to take upon itself what the Father will do, and clothe Christ in his glory, dressing him up with the brilliant garments of the consequences of his life, as if that constituted his return. That he was God in his debasement and that he will return in glory, all this is far beyond the comprehension of history; nor can all this be got from history, excepting by an incomparable lack of logic, and however incomparable one's view of history may be otherwise.

How strange, then, that one ever wished to use history in order to prove Christ divine.

d. Are the consequences of Christ's life more important than his life?

No, by no means, but rather the opposite; for else Christ were but a man.

There is really nothing remarkable in a man having lived. There have certainly lived millions upon millions of men. If the fact is remarkable, there must have been something remarkable in a man's life. In other words, there is nothing remarkable in his having lived, but his life was remarkable for this or that. The remarkable thing may, among other matters, also be what he accomplished; that is, the consequences of his life.

But that God lived here on earth in human form, that is infinitely remarkable. No matter if his life had had no consequences at all—it remains equally remarkable, infinitely remarkable, infinitely more remarkable than all possible consequences. Just try to introduce that which is remarkable as something secondary and you will straightway see the absurdity of doing so: now, if you please, whatever remarkable is there in God's life having had remarkable consequences? To speak in this fashion is merely twaddling.

No, that God lived here on earth, that is what is infinitely remarkable, that which is remarkable in itself. Assuming that Christ's life had had no consequences whatsoever—if anyone then undertook to say that therefore his life was not remarkable it would be blasphemy. For it would be remarkable all the same; and if a secondary remarkable characteristic had to be introduced it would consist in the remarkable fact that his life had no consequences. But if one should say that Christ's life was remarkable because of its consequences, then this again were a blasphemy; for it is his life which in itself is the remarkable thing.

There is nothing very remarkable in a man's having lived, but it is infinitely remarkable that God has lived. God alone can lay so much emphasis on himself that the fact of his having lived becomes infinitely more important than all the consequences which may flow therefrom and which then become a matter of history.

e. A comparison between Christ and a man who in his life endured the same treatment by his times as Christ endured.

Let us imagine a man, one of the exalted spirits, one who was wronged by his times, but whom history later reinstated in his rights by proving by the consequences of his life who he was. I do not deny, by the way, that all this business of proving from the consequences is a course well suited to "a world which ever wishes to be deceived." For he who was contemporary with him and did not understand who he was, he really only imagines that he understands when he has got to know it by help of the consequences of the noble one's life. Still, I do not wish to insist on this point, for with regard to a man it certainly holds true that the consequences of his life are more important than the fact of his having lived.

Let us imagine one of these exalted spirits. He lives among his contemporaries without being understood, his significance is not recognized—he is misunderstood, and then mocked, persecuted, and finally put to death like a common evil-doer. But the consequences of his life make it plain who he was; history which keeps a record of these consequences re-instates him in his rightful position, and now he is named in one century after another as the great and the noble spirit, and the circumstances of his debasement are almost completely forgotten. It was blindness on the part of his contemporaries which prevented them from compre-hending his true nature, and wickedness which made them mock him and deride him, and finally put him to death. But be no more concerned about this; for only after his death did he really become what he was, through the consequences of his life which, after all, are by far more im-portant than his life.

Now is it not possible that the same holds true with rega-rd to Christ? It was blindness and wickedness on the part of those times[1] but be no more concerned about this, history has now re-instated him, from history we know now who Jesus Christ was, and thus justice is done him.

---

[1] Cf. the claim of the Pharisees, Matth.23, 30: "If we had been in the days of our fathers, we would not have been partakers with them in the blood of the prophets."

Ah, wicked thoughtlessness which thus interprets Sacred history like profane history, which makes Christ a man! But can one, then, learn anything from history about Jesus? (cf. b) No, nothing. Jesus Christ is the object of faith-one either believes in him or is offended by him; for "to know" means precisely that such knowledge does not pertain to him. History can therefore, to be sure, give one knowledge in abundance; but "knowledge" annihilates Jesus Christ.

Again—ah, the impious thoughtlessness!—for one to presume to say about Christ's abasement: "Let us be concerned o more about his abasement." Surely, Christ's abasement as not something which merely happened to him—even if was the sin of that generation to crucify him; was surely not something that simply happened to him and, perhaps, would not have happened to him in better times. Christ himself w i s h e d to be abased and lowly. His abasement (that is, his walking on earth in humble guise, though being God) is therefore a condition of his own making, something he wished to be knotted together, a dialectic knot no one shall presume to untie, and which no one will for that matter, until he himself shall untie it when returning in his glory.

His case is, therefore, not the same as that of a man who, through the injustice inflicted on him by his times, was not allowed to be himself or to be valued at his worth, while history revealed who he was; for Christ himself wished to be abased—it is precisely this condition which he desired. Therefore, let history not trouble itself to do him justice, and let us not in impious thoughtlessness presumptuously imagine that we as a matter of course know who he was. For that no one knows; and he who believes it must become contemporaneous with him in his abasement. When God chooses to let himself be born in lowliness, when he who holds all possibilities in his hand assumes the form of a humble servant, when he fares about defenseless, letting people do with him what they list: he surely knows what he does and why he does it; for it is at all events he who has power over men, and not men who have power over him so let not history be so impertinent as to wish to reveal, who he was.

Lastly—ah the blasphemy!—if one should presume to say that the persecution which Christ suffered expresses something accidental! If a man is persecuted by his generation it does not follow that he has the right to say that this would happen to him in every age. Insofar there is reason in what posterity says about letting bygones be bygones. But it is different with Christ! It is not he who by letting himself be born, and by appearing in Palestine, is being examined by history; but it is he who examines, his life is the examination, not only of that generation, but of m a n k i n d. Woe unto the generation that would presumptuously dare to say: "let bygones be bygones, and forget what he suffered, for history has now revealed who he was and has done justice by him."

If one assumes that history is really able to do this, then the abasement of Christ bears an accidental relation to him; that is to say, he thereby is made a man, an extraordinary man to whom this happened through the wickedness of that generation—a fate which he was far from wishing to suffer, for he would gladly (as is human) have become a great man; whereas Christ voluntarily chose to be the lowly one and, although it was his purpose to save the world, wished also to give expression to what the "truth" suffered then, and must suffer in every generation. But if this is his strongest desire, and if he will show himself in his glory only at his return, and if he has not returned as yet; and if no generation may be without repentance, but on the contra-ry every generation must consider itself a partner in the guilt of that generation: then woe to him who presumes to deprive him of his lowliness, or to cause what he suffered to be forgotten, and to clothe him in the fabled human glory of the historic consequences of his life, which is neither here nor there.

f. The Misfortune of Christendom

But precisely this is the misfortune, and has been the misfortune, in Christendom that Christ is neither the one nor the other—neither the one he was when living on earth, nor he who will return in glory, but rather one about whom we have learned to know something in an inadmissible way from history—that he was somebody or other of great account. In an inadmissible and unlawful way we have learned to k n o w him; whereas to believe in him is the only permissible mode of approach. Men have mutually confirmed one another in the opinion that the sum total of information about him is available if they but consider the result of his life and the following 1800 years, i.e. the consequences. Gradually, as this became accepted as the truth, all pith and strength was distilled out of Christianity; the paradox was relaxed, one became a Christian without noticing it, without noticing in the least the possibility of being offended by him. One took over Christ's teachings, turned them inside out and smoothed them down—he himself guaranteeing them, of course, the man whose life had had such immense consequences in history! All became plain as day—very naturally, since Christianity in this fashion became heathendom.

Søren Kierkegaard

There is in Christendom an incessant twaddling on Sundays about the glorious and invaluable truths of Christianity, its mild consolation. But it is indeed evident that Christ lived 1800 years ago; for the rock of offense and object of faith has become a most charming fairy-story character, a kind of divine good old man.[1] People have not the remotest idea of what it means to be offended by him, and still less, what it means to worship. The qualities for which Christ is magnified are precisely those which would have most enraged one, if one had been contemporaneous with him; whereas now one feels altogether secure, placing implicit confidence in the result and, relying altogether on the verdict of history that he was the great man, concludes therefore that it is correct to do so. That is to say, it is the correct, and the noble, and the exalted, and the true, thing—if it is he who does it; which is to say, again, that one does not in any deeper sense take the pains to understand what it is he does, and that one tries even less, to the best of one's ability and with the help of God, to be like him in acting rightly and nobly, and in an exalted manner, and truthfully. For, not really fathoming it in any deeper sense, one may, in the exigency of a contemporaneous situation, judge him in exactly the opposite way. One is satisfied with admiring and extolling and is, perhaps, as was said of a translator who rendered his original word for word and therefore without making sense, "too conscientious," —one is, perhaps, also too cowardly and too weak to wish to understand his real meaning.

Christendom has done away with Christianity, without being aware of it. Therefore, if anything is to be done about it, the attempt must be made to re-introduce Christianity.

---

[1] One is here irresistibly reminded of passages in Ibsen's "Brand," e. g., Brand's conversation with Einar, in Act I. Cf. also p. 207 and Introduction p. 1.

Part II

He who invites is, then, Jesus Christ in his abasement, it is he who spoke these words of invitation. It is not from his glory that they are spoken. If that were the case, then Christianity were heathendom and the name of Christ taken in vain, and for this reason it cannot be so. But if it were the case that he who is enthroned in glory had said these words: Come hither—as though it were so altogether easy a matter to be clasped in the arms of glory—well, what wonder, then, if crowds of men ran to him! But they who thus throng to him merely go on a wild goose chase, imagining they k n o w who Christ is. But that no one k n o w s; and in order to believe in him one has to begin with his abasement.

He who invites and speaks these words, that is, he whose words they are—whereas the same words if spoken by someone else are, as we have seen, an historic falsification—he is the same lowly Jesus Christ, the humble man, born of a despised maiden, whose father is a carpenter, related to other simple folk of the very lowest class, the lowly man who at the same time (which, to be sure, is like oil poured on the fire) affirms himself to be God.

It is the lowly Jesus Christ who spoke these words. And no word of Christ, not a single one, have you permission to appropriate to yourself, you have not the least share in him, are not in any way of his company, if you have not become his contemporary in lowliness in such fashion that you have become aware, precisely like his contemporaries, of his warning: "Blessed is he whosoever shall not be offended in me."[1] You have no right to accept Christ's words, and then lie him away; you have no right to accept Christ's words, and then in a fantas-

---

[1] Matthew 11, 6.

tic manner, and with the aid of history, utterly change the nature of Christ; for the chatter of history about him is literally not worth a fig.

It is Jesus Christ in his lowliness who is the speaker. It is historically true that he said these words; but so soon as one makes a change in his historic status, it is false to say that these words were spoken by him.

This poor and lowly man, then, with twelve poor fellows as his disciples, all from the lowest class of society, for some time an object of curiosity, but later on in company only with sinners, publicans, lepers, and madmen; for one risked honor, life, and property, or at any rate (and that we know for sure) exclusion from the synagogue, by even letting one's self be helped by him—come hither n o w, all ye that labor and are heavy laden! Ah, my friend, even if you were deaf and blind and lame and leprous, if you, which has never been seen or heard before, united all human miseries in your misery—and if he wished to help you by a miracle: it is possible that (as is human) you would fear more than all your sufferings the punishment which was set on accepting aid from him, the punishment of being cast out from the society of other men, of being ridiculed and mocked, day after day, and perhaps of losing your life. It is human (and it is characteristic of being human) were you to think as follows: "no, thank you, in that case I prefer to remain deaf and blind and lame and leprous, rather than accept aid under such conditions."

"Come hither, come hither, all, ye that labor and are heavy laden, ah, come hither," lo! he invites you and opens his arms. Ah, when a gentlemanly man clad in a silken gown says this in a pleasant, harmonious voice so that the words pleasantly resound in the handsome vaulted church, a man in silk who radiates honor and respect on all who listen to him; ah, when a king in purple and velvet says this, with the Christmas tree in the background on which are hanging all the splendid gifts he intends to distribute, why, then of course there is some meaning in these words! But whatever meaning you may attach to them, so much is sure that it is not Christianity, but the exact opposite, something as diametrically opposed to Christianity as may well be; for remember who it is that invites!

And now judge for yourself—for that you have a right to do; whereas men really do not have a right to do what is so often done, viz. to deceive themselves. That a man of such appearance, a man whose company every one shuns who has the least bit of sense in his head, or the least bit to lose in the world, that he—well, this is the absurdest and maddest thing of all, one hardly knows whether to laugh or to weep about it—that he—indeed, that is the very last word one would expect to issue from his mouth, for if he had said: "Come hither and help me," or: "Leave me alone," or: "Spare me," or proudly: "I despise you all," we could understand that perfectly—but that such a man says: "Come hither to me!" why, I declare, that looks inviting indeed! And still further: "All ye that labor and are heavy laden"—as though such folk were not burdened enough with troubles, as though they now, to cap all, should be exposed to the consequences of associating with him. And then, finally: "I shall give you rest." What's that?—h e help them? Ah, I am sure even the most good-natured joker who was contemporary with him would have to say: "Surely, that was the thing he should have undertaken last of all—to wish to help others, being in that condition himself ! Why, it is about the same as if a beggar were to inform the police that he had been robbed. For it is a contradiction that one who has nothing, and has had nothing, informs us that he has been robbed; and likewise, to wish to help others when one's self needs help most." Indeed it is, humanly speaking, the most hare-brained contradiction, that he who literally "hath not where to lay his head," that he about whom it was spoken truly, in a human sense, "Behold the man!"—that he should say: "Come hither unto me all ye that suffer—I shall help!"

Now examine yourself—for that you have a right to do, You have a right to examine yourself, but you really do not have a right to let yourself without self-examination be deluded by "the others" into the belief, or to delude yourself into the belief, that you are a Christian—therefore examine yourself: supposing you were contemporary with him! True enough he—alas! he affirmed himself to be God! But many another madman has made that claim—and his times gave it as their opinion that he uttered blasphemy. Why, was not that precisely the reason why a punishment was threatened for allowing one's self to be aided by him? It was the godly care for their souls entertained by the existing order and by public opinion, lest anyone should be led astray: it was this godly care that led them to persecute him in this fashion. Therefore, before anyone resolves to be helped by him, let him consider that he must not only expect the antagonism of men, but—consider it well!—even if you could bear the consequences of that step—but consider well, that the punishment meted out by men is supposed to be God's punishment of him, "the blasphemer"—of him who invites!

Come hither n o w all ye that labor and are heavy laden!

How now? Surely this is nothing to run after—some little pause is given, which is most fittingly used to go around about by way of another street. And even if you should not thus sneak out in some way—always providing you feel yourself to be contemporary with him—or sneak into being some kind of Christian by belonging to Christendom: yet there will be a tremendous pause given, the pause which is the very condition that faith may arise: you are given pause by the possibility of being offended in him.

But in order to make it entirely clear, and bring it home to our minds, that the pause is given by him who invites, that it is he who gives us pause and renders it by no means an easy, but a peculiarly difficult, matter to follow his invitation, because one has no right to accept it without accepting also him who invites—in order to make this entirely clear I shall briefly review his life under two aspects which, to be sure, show some difference though both e s s e n t i a l l y pertain to his abasement. For it is always an abasement for God to become man, even if he were to be an emperor of emperors; and therefore he is not e s s e n t i a l l y more abased because he is a poor, lowly man, mocked, and as Scripture adds,[1] spat upon.

THE FIRST PHASE OF HIS LIFE

And now let us speak about him in a homely fashion, just as his contemporaries spoke about him, and as one speaks about some contemporary—let him be a man of the same kind as we are, whom one meets on the street in passing, of whom one knows where he lives and in what story, what his business is, who his parents are, his family, how he looks and how he dresses, with whom he associates, "and there is nothing extraordinary about him, he looks as men generally look"; in short, let us speak of him as one speaks of some contemporary about whom one does not make a great ado; for in living life together with these thousands upon thousands of r e a l people there is no room for a fine distinction like this: "Possibly, this man will be remembered in centuries to come," and "at the same time he is r e a l l y only a clerk in some shop who is no whit better than his fellows." Therefore, let us speak about him as contemporaries speak about some contemporary. I know very well what I am doing; and I want you to believe that the canting and indolent world-historic habit we have of always reverently speaking about Christ (since one has learned all

---

[1] Luke 18,32.

about it from history, and has heard so much about his having been something very extraordinary, indeed, or something of that kind)—that reverent habit, I assure you, is not worth row of pins but is, rather, sheer thoughtlessness, hypocrisy, and as such blasphemy; for it is blasphemy to reverence thoughtlessly him whom one is either to believe in or to be offended in.

It is the lowly Jesus Christ, a humble man, born of a maiden of low degree, whose father is a carpenter. To be sure, his appearance is made under conditions which are bound to attract attention to him. The small nation among whom he appears, God's Chosen People as they call themselves, live in anticipation of a Messiah who is to bring a golden period to land and people. You must grant that one form in which he appears is as different as possible from what most people would have expected. On the other hand, his appearance corresponds more to the ancient prophecies with which the people are thought to have been familiar. Thus he presents himself. A predecessor has called attention to him, and he himself fastens attention very decidedly on himself by signs and wonders which are noised abroad in all the land—and he is the hero of the hour, surrounded by unnumbered multitudes of people wheresoever he fares. The sensation aroused by him is enormous, every one's eyes are fastened on him, every one who can go about, aye even those who can only crawl, must see the wonder—and every one must have some opinion about him, so that the purveyors of ready-made opinions are put to it because the demand is so furious and the contradictions so confusing. And yet he, the worker of miracles, ever remains the humble man who literally hath not where to lay his head.

And let us not forget: signs and wonders as contemporary events have a markedly greater elasticity in repelling or attracting than the tame stories generally re-hashed by the priests, or the still tamer stories about signs and wonders that happened—1800 years ago! Signs and wonders as contemporary events are something plaguy and importunate, something which in a highly embarrassing manner almost compels one to have an opinion, something which, if one does not happen to be disposed to believe, may exasperate one excessively by thus forcing one to be contemporaneous with it. Indeed, it renders existence too complicated, and the more so, the more thoughtful, developed, and cultured one is. It is a peculiarly ticklish matter, this having to assume that a man who is contemporaneous with one really performs signs and wonders; but when he is at some distance from one, when the consequences of his life stimulate the imagination a bit, then it is not so hard to imagine, in a fashion, that one believes it.

As I said, then, the people are carried away with him; they follow him jubilantly, and see signs and wonders, both those which he performs and those which he does not perform, and they are glad in their hope that the golden age will begin, once he is king. But the crowd rarely have a clear reason for their opinions, they think one thing today and another tomorrow. Therefore the wise and the critical will not at once participate. Let us see now what the wise and the critical must think, so soon as the first impression of astonishment and surprise has subsided.

The shrewd and critical man would probably say: "Even assuming that this person is what he claims to be, that is, something extraordinary—for as to his affirming himself to be God I can, of course, not consider that as anything but an exaggeration for which I willingly make allowances, and pardon him, if I really considered him to be something extraordinary; for I am not a pedant—assuming then, which I hesitate to do, for it is a matter on which I shall at any rate suspend my judgment—assuming then that he is really performing miracles: is it not an inexplicable mystery that this person can be so foolish, so weak-minded, so altogether devoid of worldly wisdom, so feeble, or so good-naturedly vain, or whatever else you please to call it—that he behaves in this fashion and almost forces his benefactions on men? Instead of proudly and commandingly keeping people away from himself at a distance marked by their profoundest submission, whenever he does allow himself to be seen, at rare occasions: instead of doing so, think of his being accessible to everyone, or rather himself going to everyone, of having intercourse with everybody, almost as if being the extraordinary person consisted in his being everybody's servant,[1] as if the extraordinary person he claims to be were marked by his being concerned only lest men should fail to be benefited by him—in short as if being an extraordinary person consisted in being the most solicitous of all persons. The whole business is inexplicable to me—what he wants, what his purpose is, what end he has in mind, what he expects to accomplish; in a word, what the meaning of it all is. He who by so many a wise saying reveals so profound an insight into the human heart, he must certainly know what I, using but half of my wits, can predict for him, viz. that in such fashion one gets nowhere in the

---

[1] Matthew 20, 27f.

world—unless, indeed, despising prudence, one consistently aims to make a fool of one's self or, perchance, goes so far in sincerity as to prefer being put to death; but anyone desiring that must certainly be crazy. Having such profound knowledge of the human heart he certainly ought to know that the thing to do is to deceive people and then to give one's deception the appearance of being a benefaction conferred on the whole race. By doing so one reaps all advantages, even the one whose enjoyment is the sweetest of all, which is, to be called by one's contemporaries a benefactor of the human race—for, once in your grave, you may snap your fingers at what posterity may have to say about you. But to surrender one's self altogether, as he does, and not to think the least of one's self—in fact, almost to beg people to accept these benefactions: no, I would not dream of joining his company. And, of course, neither does he invite me; for, indeed, he invites only them that labor and are heavy laden."

Or he would reason as follows: "His life is simply a fantastic dream. In fact, that is the mildest expression one can use about it; for, when judging him in this fashion, one is good-natured enough to forget altogether the evidence of sheer madness in his claim to be God. This is wildly fantastical. One may possibly live a few years of one's youth in such fashion. But he is now past thirty years. And he is literally nothing. Still further, in a very short time he will necessarily lose all the respect and reputation he has gained among the people, the only thing, you may say, he has gained for himself. One who wishes to keep in the good graces of the people—the riskiest chance imaginable, I will admit—he must act differently. Not many months will pass before the crowd will grow tired of one who is so altogether at their service. He will be regarded as a ruined person, a kind of outcast, who ought to be glad to end his days in a corner, the world forgetting, by the world forgot; providing he does not, by continuing his previous behavior, prefer to maintain his present attitude and be fantastic enough to wish to be put to death, which is the unavoidable consequence of persevering in that course. What has he done for his future? Nothing. Has he any assured position? No. What expectations has he? None. Even this trifling matter: what will he do to pass the time when he grows older, the long winter nights, what will he do to make them pass—why, he cannot even play cards! He is now enjoying a bit of popular favor—in truth, of all movable property the most movable—which in a trice may turn into an enormous popular hatred of him.—Join his company? No, thank you, I am still, thank God, in my right mind.

Søren Kierkegaard

Or he may reason as follows: "That there is something extraordinary about this person—even if one reserves the right, both one's own and that of common sense, to refrain from venturing any opinion as to his claim of being God—about that there is really little doubt. Rather, one might be indignant at Providence's having entrusted such a person with these powers—a person who does the very opposite what he himself bids us do: that we shall not cast our pearls before the swine; for which reason he will, as he himself predicts, come to grief by their turning about and trampling him under their feet. One may always expect this of swine; but, on the other hand, one would not expect that he who had himself called attention to this likelihood, himself would do precisely[1] what he knows one should not do. If only there were some means of cleverly stealing his wisdom—for I shall gladly leave him in undisputed possession of that very peculiar thought of his that he is God—if one could but rob his wisdom without, at the same time, becoming his disciple! If one could only steal up to him at night and lure it from him; for I am more than equal to editing and publishing it, and better than he, if you please. I undertake to astonish the whole world by getting something altogether different out of it; for I clearly see there is something wondrously profound in what he says, and the misfortune is only that he is the man he is. But perhaps, who knows, perhaps it is feasible, anyway, to fool him out of it. Perhaps in that respect too he is good—natured and simple enough to communicate it quite freely to me. It is not impossible; for it seems to me that the wisdom he unquestionably possesses, evidently has been entrusted to a fool, seeing there is so much contradiction in his life.—But as to joining his company and becoming his disciple—no indeed, that would be the same as becoming a fool oneself."

Or he might reason as follows: "If this person does indeed mean to further what is good and true (I do not venture to decide this), he is helpful at least, in this respect, to Youths and inexperienced people. For they will be benefited, in this serious life of ours, by learning, the sooner the better, and very thoroughly—he opens the eyes even of the blindest to this—that all this pretense of wishing to live only for goodness and truth contains a considerable admixture of the ridiculous. He proves how right the poets of our times are when they let truth and goodness be represented by some half-witted fellow, one who is so stupid that you can knock down a wall with him. The idea of exerting

---

[1] The original here does not agree with the sense of the passage.

one's self, as this man does, of renouncing everything but pains and trouble, to be at beck and call all day long, more eager than the busiest family physician—and pray why? Because he makes a living by it? No, not in the very least; it has never occurred to him, as far as I can see, to want something in in return. Does he earn any money by it? No, not a red cent—he has not a red cent to his name, and if he did he would forthwith give it away. Does he, then, aspire to a position of honor and dignity in the state? On the contrary, he loathes all worldly honor. And he who, as I said, condemns all worldly honor, and practices the art of living on nothing; he who, if any one, seems best fitted to pass his life in a most comfortable dolce far niente—which is not such a bad thing—: he lives under a greater strain than any government official who is rewarded by honor and dignity, lives under a greater strain than any business man who earns money like sand. Why does he exert himself thus, or (why this question about a matter not open to question?) why should anyone exert himself thus—in order to attain to the happiness of being ridiculed, mocked, and so forth? To be sure, a peculiar kind of pleasure! That one should push one's way through a crowd to reach the spot where money, honor, and glory are distributed—why, that is perfectly understandable; but to push forward to be whipped: how exalted, how Christian, how stupid!"

Or he will reason as follows: "One hears so many rash opinions about this person from people who understand nothing—and worship him; and so many severe condemnations of him by those who, perhaps, misunderstand him after all. As for me, I am not going to allow myself to be accused of venturing a hasty opinion. I shall keep entirely cool and calm; in fact, which counts for still more, I am conscious of being as reasonable and moderate with him as is possible. Grant now—which, to be sure, I do only to a certain extent—grant even that one's reason is impressed by this person. What, then, is my opinion about him? My opinion is, that for the present, I can form no opinion about him. I do not mean about his claim of being God; for about that I can never in all eternity have an opinion. No, I mean about him as a man. Only by the consequences of his life shall we be able to decide whether he was an extraordinary person or whether, deceived by his imagination, he applied too high a standard, not only to himself, but also to humanity in general. More I cannot do for him, try as I may—if he were my only friend, my own child, I could not judge him more leniently, nor differently, either. It follows from this, to be sure, that in all probability, and for good reasons, I shall not ever be able to have any opinion about him. For in order to be able to form an opinion I

Søren Kierkegaard

must first see the consequences of his life, including his very last moments; that is, he must be dead then, and perhaps not even then, may I form an opinion of him. And, even granting this, it is not really an opinion about him, for he is then no more. No more is needed to say why it is impossible for me to join him while he is living. The a u t h o r i t y he is said to show in his teaching can have no decisive influence in my case; for it is surely easy to see that his thought moves in a circle. He quotes as authority that which he is to prove, which in its turn can be proved only by the consequences of his life; provided, of course, it is not connected with that fixed idea of his about being God, because if it is t h e r e f o r e he has this authority (because he is God) the answer must be: yes—if! So much, however, I may admit, that if I could imagine myself living in some later age, and if the consequences of his life as shown in history had made it plain that he was the extraordinary person he in a former age claimed to be, then it might very well be—in fact, I might come very near, becoming his disciple."

An ecclesiastic would reason as follows: "For an impostor and demagogue he has, to say the truth, a remarkable air of honesty about him; for which reason he cannot be so absolutely dangerous, either, even though the situation looks dangerous enough while the squall is at its height, and ever, though the situation looks dangerous enough with his enormous popularity—until the squall has passed over and the people—yes, precisely the people—overthrow him again. The honest thing about him is his claim to be the Messiah when he resembles him so little as he does. That is honest, just as if someone in preparing bogus paper-money made the bills so poorly that everyone who knows the least about it cannot fail to detect the fraud.—True enough, we all look forward to a Messiah, but surely no one with any sense expects God himself to come, and every religious person shudders at the blasphemous attitude of this person. We look forward to a Messiah, we are all agreed on that. But the governance of the world does not go forward tumultuously, by leaps and bounds; the development of the world, as is indicated by the very fact that it is a development, proceeds by evolution, not by revolution. The true Messiah will therefore look quite different, and will arrive as the most glorious flower, and the highest development, of that which already exists. Thus will the true Messiah come, and he will proceed in an entirely different fashion: he will recognize the existing order as the basis of things, he will summon all the clergy to council and present to them the results accomplished by him, as well as his credentials—and then, if he obtain the majority of the votes when the ballot is cast, he will be received and saluted as the extraordinary person, as the one he is: the Messiah.[1]

"However, there is a duplicity in this man's behavior; he assumes too much the rôle of judge. It seems as if he wished to be, at one and the same time, both the judge who passes sentence on the existing order of things, and the Messiah. If he does not wish to play the rôle of the judge, then why his absolute isolation, his keeping at a distance from all which has to do with the existing order of things? And if he does not wish to be the judge, then why his fantastic flight from reality to join the ignorant crowd, then why with the haughtiness of a revolutionary does he despise all the intelligence and efficiency to be found in the existing order of things? And why does he begin afresh altogether, and absolutely from the bottom up, by the help of—fishermen and artisans? May not the fact that he is an illegitimate child fitly characterize his entire relation to the existing order of things? On the other hand, if he wishes to be only the Messiah, why then his warning about putting a piece of new cloth unto an old garment.[2] For these words are precisely the watchwords of every revolution since they are expressive of a person's discontent with the existing order and of his wish to destroy it. That is, these words reveal his desire to remove existing conditions, rather than to build on them and better them, if one is a reformer, or to develop them to their highest possibility, if one is indeed the Messiah. This is duplicity. In fact, it is not feasible to be both judge and Messiah. Such duplicity will surely result in his downfall.[3] The climax in the life of a judge is his death by violence, and so the poet pictures it correctly; but the climax in the life of the Messiah cannot possibly be his death. Or else, by that very fact, he would not be the Messiah, that is, he whom the existing order expects in order to deify him. This duplicity has not as yet been recognized by the people, who see in him their Messiah; but the existing order of things cannot by any manner of means recognize him as such. The people, the idle and loafing crowd, can do so only because they represent nothing less than the existing order of things. But as soon as the duplicity becomes evident to them, his doom is sealed. Why, in this respect his predecessor was a far more definitely marked personality, for he was but one

---

[1] Björnson's play of "Beyond Human Power," Part I, Act 2, reads like an elaboration of these views.
[2] Matthew 9, 16.
[3] The following passage is capable of different interpretations in the original.

thing, the judge. But what confusion and thoughtlessness, to wish to be both, and what still worse confusion, to acknowledge his predecessor as the judge—that is, in other words, precisely to make the existing order of things receptive and ripe for the Messiah who is to come after the judge, and yet not wish to associate himself with the existing order of things!"

And the philosopher would reason as follows: "Such dreadful or, rather, insane vanity, that a single individual claims to be God, is a thing hitherto unheard of. Never before have we been witness to such an excess of pure subjectivity and sheer negation. He has no doctrines, no system of philosophy, he knows really nothing, he simply keeps on repeating, and making variations on, some unconnected aphoristic sentences, some few maxims, and a couple of parables by which he dazzles the crowd for whom he also performs signs and wonders; so that they, instead of learning something, or being improved, come to believe in one who in a most brazen way constantly forces his subjective views on us. There is nothing objective or positive whatever in him and in what he says. Indeed, from a philosophical point of view, he does not need to fear destruction for he has perished already, since it is inherent in the nature of subjectivity to perish. One may in all fairness admit that his subjectivity is remarkable and that, be it as it may with the other miracles, he constantly repeats his miracle with the five small loaves,[1] viz., by means of a few lyric utterances and some aphorisms he rouses the whole country. But even if one were inclined to overlook his insane notion of affirming himself to be God, it is an incomprehensible mistake, which, to be sure, demonstrates a lack of philosophic training, to believe that God could reveal himself in the form of an individual. The race, the universal, the total, is God; but the race surely is not an individual! Generally speaking, that is the impudent assumption of subjectivity, which claims that the individual is something extraordinary. But sheer insanity is shown in the claim of an individual to be God. Because if the insane thing were possible, viz. that an individual might be God, why, then this individual would have to be worshipped, and a more beastly philosophic stupidity is not conceivable."

The astute statesman would reason as follows: "That at present this person wields great power is undeniable—entirely disregarding, of course, this notion of his that he is God. Foibles like these, being idio-

---

[1] Matthew 14, 17.

syncrasies, do not count against a man and concern no one, least of all a statesman. A statesman is concerned only with what power a man wields; and that he does wield great power cannot, as I have remarked, be denied. But what he intends to do, what his aim is, I cannot make out at all. If this be calculation it must be of an entirely new and peculiar order, not so altogether unlike what is otherwise called madness. He possesses points of considerable strength; but he seems to defeat, rather than to use, it; he expends it without h i m s e l f getting any returns. I consider him a phenomenon with which—as ought to be one's rule with all phenomena—a wise man should not have anything to do, since it is impossible to calculate him or the catastrophe threatening his life. It is possible that he will be made king. It is possible, I say; but it is not impossible, or rather, it is just as possible, that he may end on the gallows. He lacks earnestness in all his endeavors. With all his enormous stretch of wings he only hovers and gets nowhere. He does not seem to have any definite plan of procedure, but just hovers. Is it for his nationality he is fighting, or does he aim at a communistic revolution? Does he wish to establish a republic or a kingdom? With which party does he affiliate himself to combat which party, or does he wish to fight all parties ?

"I have anything to do with him?—No, that would be the very last thing to enter my mind. In fact, I take all possible precautions to avoid him. I keep quiet, undertake nothing, act as if I did not exist; for one cannot even calculate how he might interfere with one's undertakings, be they

ever so unimportant, or at any rate, how one might become involved in the vortex of his activities. Dangerous, in a certain sense enormously dangerous, is this man. But I calculate that I may ensnare him precisely by doing nothing. For overthrown he must be. And this is done most safely by letting him do it himself, by letting him stumble over himself. I have, at least at this moment, not sufficient power to bring about his fall; in fact, I know no one who has. To undertake the least thing against him now, means to be crushed one's self. No, my plan is constantly to exert only negative resistance to him, that is, to do nothing, and he will probably involve himself in the enormous consequences he draws after him, till in the end he will tread on his own train, as it were, and thus fall."

And the steady citizen would reason as follows (which would then become the opinion of his family) : "Now, let us be human, everything is good when done in moderation, too little and too much spoil everything, and as a French saying has it which I once heard a traveling salesman use: every power which exceeds itself comes to a fall—and as to this person, his fall is certainly sure enough. I have earnestly spoken to my son and warned and admonished him not to drift into evil ways and join that person. And why? Because all people are running after him. That is to say, what sort of people? Idlers and loafers, street-walkers and tramps, who run after everything. But mightily few of the men who have house and property, and nobody who is wise and respected, none after whom I set my clock, neither councillor Johnson, nor senator Anderson, nor the wealthy broker Nelson—oh no! they know what's what. And as to the ministry who ought to know most about such matters—ah, they will have none of him. What was it pastor Green said in the club the other evening? 'That man will yet come to a terrible end,' he said. And Green, he can do more than preach, you oughtn't to hear him Sundays in church so much as Mondays in the club—I just wished I had half his knowledge of affairs! He said quite correctly, and as if spoken out of my own heart: 'Only idlers and loafers are running after that man.' And why do they run after him? Because he performs some miracles. But who is sure they are miracles, or that he can confer the same power on his disciples? And, in any case, a miracle is something mightily uncertain, whereas the certain is the certain. Every serious father who has grown-up children must be truly alarmed lest his sons be seduced and join that man together with the desperate characters who follow him—desperate characters who have nothing to lose. And even these, how does he help them? Why, one must be mad to wish to be helped in this fashion. Even the poorest beggar is brought to a worse estate than his former one, is brought to a pass he could have escaped by remaining what he was, that is, a beggar and no more."

And the mocker, not the one hated on account of his malice, but the one who is admired for his wit and liked for his good nature, he would reason as follows: "It is, after all, a rich idea which is going to prove useful to all of us, that an individual who is in no wise different from us claims to be God. If that is not being a benefactor of the race then I don't know what charity and beneficence are. If we assume that the characteristic of being God—well, who in all the world would have hit on that idea? How true that such an idea could not have entered into the heart of man[1]—but if we assume that it consists in looking in no wise different from the rest of us, and in nothing else: why, then we

---

[1] Cf. 1 Cor. 2, 9.

are all gods. Q. E. D. Three cheers for him, the inventor of a discovery so extraordinarily important for mankind! Tomorrow I, the undersigned, shall proclaim that I am God, and the discoverer at least will not be able to contradict me without contradicting himself. At night all cats are gray; and if to be God consists in looking like the rest of us, absolutely and altogether like the rest of mankind: why, then it is night and we all are . . ., or what is it I wanted to say: we all are God, every one of us, and no one has a right to say he isn't as well off as his neighbor. This is the most ridiculous situation imaginable, the contradiction here being the greatest, imaginable, and a contradiction always making for a comical effect. But this is in no wise my discovery, but solely that of the discoverer: this idea that a man of exactly the same appearance as the rest of us, only not half so well dressed as the average man, that is, a poorly dressed person who, rather than being God, seems to invite the attention of the society for the relief of the poor—that he is God! I am only sorry for the director of the charitable society that he will not get a raise from this general advancement of the human race but that he will, rather, lose his job on account of this, etc."

Ah, my friend, I know well what I am doing, I know my responsibility, and my soul is altogether assured of the correctness of my procedure. Now then, imagine yourself a contemporary of him who invites. Imagine yourself to be a sufferer, but consider well to what you expose yourself in becoming his disciple and following him. You expose yourself to losing practically everything in the eyes of all wise and sensible and respected men. He who invites demands of you that you surrender all, give up everything; but the common sense of your own times and of your contemporaries will not give you up, but will judge that to join him is madness. And mockery will descend cruelly upon you; for while it will almost spare him, out of compassion, you will be thought madder than a march-hare for becoming his disciple. People will say: "That h e is a wrong-headed enthusiast, that can't be helped. Well and good; but to become—in all seriousness—his disciple, that is the greatest piece of madness imaginable. There surely is but one possibility of being madder than a madman, which is the higher madness of joining a madman in all seriousness and regarding him as a sage."

Do not say that the whole presentation above is exaggerated. Ah, you know (but, possibly, have not fully realized it) that among all the respectable men, among all the enlightened and sensible men, there was but one—though it is easily possible that one or the other of them, impelled by curiosity, entered into conversation with him—that there was but one among them who sought him in all seriousness.[1] And he came to him—in the night! And as you know, in the night one walks on forbidden paths, one chooses the night to go to places of which one does not like to be known as a frequenter. Consider the opinion of the inviter implied in this—it was a disgrace to visit him, something no man of honor could afford to do, as little as to pay a nightly visit to—but no, I do not care to say in so many words what would follow this "as little as."

Come hither to me now all ye that labor and are heavy laden, and I will give you rest.

THE SECOND PHASE OF HIS LIFE

His end was what all the wise and the sensible, the statesmen and the citizens and the mockers, etc., predicted it would be. And as was later spoken to him, in a moment when, it would seem, the most hardened ought to have been moved to sympathy, and the very stones to tears: "He saved others; let him save himself,"[2] and as it has been repeated thousands upon thousands of times, by thousands upon thousands: "What was it he spoke of before, saying his hour was not yet come[3]—is it come now, perchance?"—It has been repeated, alas, the while the single individual, the believer, shudders whenever considering—while yet unable to refrain from gazing into the depth of what to men is a meaningless absurdity—shudders when considering that God in human guise, that his divine teaching, that these signs and wonders which might have made a very Sodom and Gomorrha reform its ways, in reality produced the exact opposite, and caused the teacher to be shunned, hated, despised.

Who he is, one can recognize more easily now when the powerful ones and the respected ones, and all the precautionary measures of those upholding the existing order, have corrected any wrong conception one might have entertained about him at first—now when the people have lost their patience to wait for a Messiah, seeing that his life, instead of rising in dignity, lapsed into ever greater degradation. Who, pray, does not recognize that a man is judged according to the society in which he moves—and now, think of his society! Indeed, his

---

[1] John 3, 1f.
[2] Luke 23, 35.
[3] John 2, 4, etc.

society one might well designate as equivalent to being expelled from "human society"; for his society are the lowest classes of the people, with sinners and publicans among them, people whom everybody with the slightest self-respect shuns for the sake of his good name and reputation—and a good name and reputation surely are about the least one can wish to preserve. In his company there are, furthermore, lepers whom every one flees, madmen who can only inspire terror, invalids and wretches—squalor and misery. Who, then, is this person that, though followed by such a company, still is the object of the persecution of the mighty ones? He is one despised as a seducer of men, an impostor, a blasphemer! And if anyone enjoying a good reputation refrains from expressing contempt of him, it is really only a kind of compassion; for to fear him is, to be sure, something different.

Such, then, is his appearance; for take care not to be influenced by anything that you may have learned after the event—as, how his exalted spirit, with an almost divine majesty, never was so markedly manifest as just them. Ah, my friend, if you were the contemporary of one who is not only himself "excluded from the synagogue" but, as you will remember, whose very help meant being "excluded from the synagogue"—I say, if you were the contemporary of an outcast, who in every respect answers to that term, (for everything has two sides) : then you will scarcely be the man to explain all this in terms directly contrary to appearances;[1] or, which is the same thing, you will not be the "single individual" which, as you well know, no one wants to be, and to be which is regarded as a ridiculous oddity, perhaps even as a crime.

And now—for they are his society chiefly—as to his apostles! What absurdity; though not—what new absurdity, for it is quite in keeping with the rest—his apostles are some fishermen, ignorant people who but the other day followed their trade. And tomorrow, to pile one absurdity on the other, they are to go out into the wide world and transform its aspect. And it is he who claims to be God, and these are his duly appointed apostles! Now, is he to make his apostles respected, or are perhaps the apostles to make him respected? Is he, the inviter, is he an absurd dreamer? Indeed, his procession would make it seem so; no poet -could have hit on a better idea. A teacher, a sage, or whatever you please to call him, a kind of stranded genius, who af-

---

[1] The passage is not quite clear. Probably, you will not be the man to explain this phenomenon in the very opposite terms, viz., as the divinity himself.

firms himself to be God—surrounded by a jubilant mob, himself accompanied by some publicans, criminals, and lepers; nearest to him a chosen few, his apostles. And these judges so excellently competent as to what truth is, these fishermen, tailors, and shoe-makers, they do not only admire him, their teacher and master, whose every word is wisdom and truth; they do not only see what no one else can see, his exaltedness and holiness, nay, but they see God in him and worship him. Certainly, no poet could invent a better situation, and it is doubtful if the poet would not forget the additional item that this same person is feared by the mighty ones and that they are scheming to destroy him. His death alone can reassure and satisfy them. They have set an ignominious punishment on joining his company, on merely accepting aid from him; and yet they do not feel secure, and cannot feel altogether reassured that the whole thing is mere wrongheaded enthusiasm and absurdity. Thus the mighty ones. The populace who had idolized him, the populace have pretty nearly given him up, only in moments does their old conception of him blaze forth again. In all his existence there is not a shred the most envious of the envious might envy him to have. Nor do the mighty ones envy his life. They demand his death for safety's sake, so that they may have peace again, when all has returned to the accustomed ways, peace having been made still more secure by the warning example of his death.

These are the two phases of his life. It began with the people's idolizing him, whereas all who were identified with the existing order of things, all who had power and influence, vengefully, but in a cowardly and hidden manner, laid their snares for him—in which he was caught, then? Yes, but he perceived it well. Finally the people discover that they had been deceived in him, that the fulfillment he would bring them answered least of all to their expectations of wonders and mountains of gold. So the people deserted him and the mighty ones drew the snare about him—in which he was caught, then? Yes, but he perceived it well. The mighty ones drew the snare together about him—and thereupon the people, who then saw themselves completely deceived, turned against him in hatred and rage.

And—to include that too—compassion would say; or, among the compassionate one—for compassion is sociable, and likes to assemble together, and you will find spitefulness and envy keeping company with whining soft-headedness: since, as a heathen philosopher observed long ago, no one is so ready to sympathize as an envious person—among the compassionate ones the verdict would be: it is really too bad that this good-hearted fellow is to come to such an end.

For he was really a good sort of fellow. Granting it was an exaggeration to claim to be God, he really was good to the poor and the needy, even if in an odd manner, by becoming one of them and going about in the company of beggars. But there is something touching in it all, and one can't help but feel sorry for the poor fellow who is to suffer such a miserable death. For you may say what you will, and condemn him as strongly as you will, I cannot help feeling pity for him. I am not so heard-hearted as not to feel compassion."

We have arrived at the last phase, not of Sacred History, as handed down by the apostles and disciples who believed in Christ, but of profane history, its counterpart.

Come hither now, all ye that labor and are heavy laden: that is, if you feel the need, even if you are of all sufferers the most miserable— if you feel the need of being helped in this fashion, that is, to fall into still greater suffering, then come hither, he will help you.

Part III

THE INVITATION AND THE INVITER

Let us forget for a little while what, in the strictest sense, constitutes the "offense"; which is, that the inviter claims to be God. Let us assume that he did not claim to be more than a man, and let us then consider the inviter and his invitation.

The invitation is surely inviting enough. How, then, shall one explain the bad relation which did exist, this terribly wrong relation, that no one, or practically no one, accepted the invitation; that, on the contrary, all, or practically all—alas! and was it not precisely all who were invited?—that practically all were at one in offering resistance to the inviter, in wishing to put him to death, and in setting a punishment on accepting aid from him? Should one not expect that after an invitation such as he issued all, all who suffered, would come crowding to him, and that all they who were not suffering would crowd to him, touched by the thought of such compassion and mercy, and that thus the whole race would be at one in admiring and extolling the inviter? How is the opposite to be explained? For that this was the outcome is certain enough; and the fact that it all happened in those remote times is surely no proof that the generation then living was worse than other generations! How could anyone be so thoughtless as to believe that? For whoever gives any thought to the matter will easily see that it happened in that generation only because they chanced to be contemporaneous with him. How then explain that it happened—that all came to that terribly wrong end, so opposite to what ought to have been expected?

Well, in the first place, if the inviter had looked the figure which purely human compassion would have him be; and, in the second place, if he had entertained the purely human conception of what constitutes man's misery—why, then it would probably not have happened.

In the first place: According to this human conception of him he should have been a most generous and sympathetic person, and at the same time possessed of all qualifications requisite for being able to help in all troubles of this world, ennobling the help thus extended by a profound and heartfelt human compassion. Withal (so they would imagine him) he should also have been a man of some distinction and not without a certain amount of human self-assertion—the consequence of which would be, however, that he would neither have been able, in his compassion, to reach down to all sufferers, nor yet to have comprehended, fully what constitutes the misery of man and of mankind.

But divine compassion, the infinite u n c o n c e r n which takes thought only of those that suffer, and not in the least of one's self, and which with absolute unconcern takes thought of all that suffer: that will always seem to men only a kind of madness, and they will ever be puzzled whether to laugh or to weep about it. Even if nothing else had militated against the inviter, this alone would have been sufficient to make his lot hard in the world.

Let a man but try a little while to practice divine compassion, that is, to be somewhat unconcerned in his compassion., and you will at once perceive what the opinion of mankind would be. For example: let one who could occupy some higher rank in society, let him not (preserving all the while the distinction of his position) lavishly give to the poor, and philanthropically (i.e. in a superior fashion) visit the poor and the sick and the wretched—no, let him give up altogether the distinction of his position and in all earnest choose the company of the poor and the lowly, let him live altogether with the people, with workmen, hodmen, mortarmixers, and the like! Ah, in a quiet moment, when not actually b e h o l d i n g him, most of us will be moved to tears by the mere thought of it; but no sooner would they s e e him in this company—him who might have attained to honor and dignity in the world—see him walking along in such goodly company, with a bricklayer's apprentice on his right side and a cobbler's boy on his left, but—well, what then? First they would devise a thousand explanations to explain that it is because of queer notions, or obstinacy, or pride, or vanity that he chooses this mode of life. And even if they would refrain from attributing to him these evil motives they will never be reconciled with the sight of him—in this company. The noblest person in the world will be tempted to laugh, the moment he s e e s it.

Søren Kierkegaard

And if all the clergymen in the world, whether in velvet or in silk or in broadcloth or in satin, contradicted me I would say: "You lie, you only deceive people with your Sunday sermons. Because it will always be possible for a contemporary to say about one so compassionate (who, it is to be kept in mind, is our contemporary): "I believe he is actuated by vanity, and that is why I laugh and mock at him; but if he were truly compassionate, or had I been contemporary with him, the noble one—why then!" And now, as to those exalted ones "who were not understood by men"—to speak in the fashion of the usual run of sermons—why, sure enough, they are dead. In this fashion these people succeed in playing hide and seek. You simply assume that every contemporary who ventures out so far is actuated only by vanity; and as to the departed, you assume that they are dead and that they, therefore, were among the glorious ones.

It must be remembered, to be sure, that every person, wishes to maintain his own level in life, and this fixed point, this steady endeavor, is one of the causes which limit h u m a n compassion to a certain sphere. The cheesemonger will think that to live like the inmate of a poorhouse is going too far in expressing one's sympathy; for the sympathy of the cheese-monger is biased in one regard which is, his regard of the opinion of other cheese-mongers and of the saloon-keepers. His compassion is therefore not without its limitations. And thus with every class—and the journalists, living as they do on the pennies of the poor, under the pretense of asserting and defending their rights, they would be the first to heap ridicule on this unlimited compassion.

To identify one's self wholly and literally with him who is most miserable (and this, only this, is d i v i n e compassion), that is to men the "too much" by which one is moved to tears, in a quiet Sunday hour, and about which one unconsciously bursts into laughter when one sees it in r e a l i t y. The fact is, it is too exalted a sight for daily use; one must have it at some distance to be able to support it. Men are not so familiar with exalted virtue to believe it at once. The contradiction seen here is, therefore, that this exalted virtue manifests itself in-reality, in daily life, quite literally the daily life. When the poet or the orator illustrates this exalted virtue, that is, pictures it in a poetical distance from real life, men are moved; but to see this exalted virtue in reality, the reality of daily life, here in Copenhagen, on the Market Square, in the midst of busy every-day life-! And when the poet or the orator does touch people it is only for a short time, and just so long are men able to believe, almost, in this exalted virtue. But to see it in real life every day-! To be sure, there is an enormous contradiction in the statement that the most exalted of all has become the most every-day occurrence!

Insofar, then, it was certain in advance what would be the inviter's fate, even if nothing else had contributed to his doom. The absolute,[1] or all which makes for an absolute standard, becomes by that very fact the victim. For men are willing enough to practice sympathy and self-denial, are willing enough to strive for wisdom, etc.; but they wish themselves to determine the standard and to have that read: "to a certain degree." They do not wish to do away with all these splendid virtues. On the contrary, they want-at a bargain and in all comfort-to have the appearance and the name of practicing them. Truly divine compassion is therefore necessarily the victim so soon as it shows itself in this world. It descends on earth out of compassion for mankind, and yet it is mankind who trample upon it. And whilst it is wandering about among them, scarcely even the

sufferer dares to flee to it, for fear of mankind. The fact is, it is most important for the world to keep up the appearance of being compassionate; but this it made out by divine compassion to be a falsehood-and therefore: away with divine compassion!

But now the inviter represented precisely this divine compassion-and therefore he was sacrificed, and therefore even those that suffered fled from him; for they comprehended (and, humanly speaking, very exactly), what is true of most human infirmities, that one is better off to remain what one is than to be helped by him.

In the second place: the inviter likewise had another, and altogether different, conception than the purely human one as to what constitutes man's misery. And in this sense only he was intent on helping; for he had with him neither money, nor medicine, nor anything else of this kind.

Indeed, the inviter's appearance is so altogether different from what human compassion would imagine it that he is a downright offense to men. In a purely human sense there is something positively cruel-something outrageous, something so exasperating as to make one wish to kill that person-in the fact of his inviting to him the poor and the 'sick and the suffering, and then not being able to do anything for them, except to promise them remission of their sins. "Let us be human, man is no spirit. And when a person is about to die of starvation

---

[1] Here, the unreserved identification with human suffering above referred to.

and you say to him: I promise you the gracious remission of your sins-that is revolting cruelty. In fact it is ridiculous, though too serious a matter to laugh about."

Well (for in quoting these sentiments I wish merely to let offended man discover the contradiction and exaggerate it-it is not I who wish to exaggerate), well then, the real intention of the inviter was to point out that sin is the destruction of mankind. Behold now, that makes room, as the invitation also made room, almost as if he had said procul, o procul este profani, or as if, even though he had not said it, a voice had been heard which thus interpreted the "come hither" of the invitation. There surely are not many sufferers who will follow the invitation. And ever, if there were one who, although aware that from this inviter no actual worldly help was to be expected, nevertheless had sought refuge with him, touched by his compassion: now even he will flee from him. For is it not almost a bit of sharp practice to profess to be here out of compassion, and then to speak about sin?

Indeed, it is a piece of cunning, unless you are altogether certain that you are a sinner. If it is tooth-ache which bothers you, or if your house is burned to the ground, but if it has escaped you that you are a sinner-why, then it was cunning on his part. It is a bit of sharp practice of him to assert: "I heal all manner of disease," in order to say, when one approaches him: "the fact is, I recognize only one disease, which is sin-of that I shall cure all them 'that labor and are heavy laden,' all them that labor to work themselves free of the power of sin, that labor to resist the evil, and to vanquish their weakness, but succeed only in being laden." Of this malady he cures "all" persons; even if there were but a single one who turned to him because of this malady: he heals all persons. But to come to him on account of any other disease, and only because of that, is about as useful as to look up an eye-doctor when you have fractured your leg.

CHRISTIANITY AS THE ABSOLUTE; CONTEMPORANEOUSNESS WITH CHRIST

With its invitation to all "that labor and are heavy laden" Christianity has entered the world, not-as the clergy whimperingly and falsely introduce it-as a shining paragon of mild grounds of consolation; but as the absolute. God wills it so because of His love, but it is God who wills it, and He wills it as He wills it. He does not choose to have His nature changed by man and become a nice, that is to say, humane, God; but He chooses to change the nature of man because of His love for them. Neither does He care to hear any human impertinence concerning the why and wherefore of Christianity, and why it entered the world: it is, and is to be, the absolute. Therefore all the relative explanations which may have been ventured as to its why and wherefore are entirely beside the point. Possibly, these explanations were suggested by a kind of human compas-sion which believes it necessary to haggle a bit-God very likely does not know the nature of man very well, His de-mands are a bit exorbitant, and therefore the clergymen just haggle and beat Him down a bit.[1] Maybe the clergy hit upon that idea in order to stand well with men and reap some advantage from preaching the gospel; for if its de-mands are reduced to the purely human, to the de-mands which arise in man's heart, why, then men will of course think well of it, and of course also of the amiable preacher who knows how to make Christianity so mild-if the Apostl-es had been able to do that the world would have esteemed them highly also in their time. However, all this is the absolute. But what is it good for, then-is it not a downright torment? Why, yes, you may say so: from the stand-point of the relative, the absolute is the greatest torment. In his dull, languid, sluggish moments, when man is domin-ated by his sensual nature, Christianity is an absurdity to him since it is not commensurable with any definite "wherefore?" But of what use is it, then? Answer: peace! it is the absolute. And thus it must be represented; that is, in a fashion which makes it appear as an absurdity to the sensual nature of man. And therefore is it, ah, so true and, in still another sense, so true when the worldly--wise man who is contemporaneous with Christ condemns him with the words: "he is literally nothing"--quite true, for he is the absolute. And, being absolute, Christianity has come in the world, not as a consolation in the human sense; in fact, quite on the contrary, it is ever reminding one how the Christian must suffer in order to become, or to remain, a Christian-sufferings which he may, if you please, escape by not electing to be a Christian.

    There is, indeed, an unbridgeable gulf fixed between God and man. It therefore became plain to those contemporary with Christ that the process of becoming a Christian (that is, being changed into the likeness of God) is, in a human sense, a greater torment and wretchedness and pain than the greatest conceivable human suffering, and moreover

---

[1] Cf. Note p. 178.

a crime in the eyes of one's contemporaries. And thus will it always be; that is, if becoming a Christian in reality means becoming contemporaneous with Christ. And if becoming a Christian does not have that meaning, then all your chatter about becoming a Christian is a vanity, a delusion and a snare, and likewise a blasphemy and a sin against the Holy Ghost.

For with regard to the absolute there is but one time, viz. the present. He who is not contemporaneous with the absolute, for him it does not exist at all. And since Christ is the absolute, it is evident that in respect of him there is but one situation: contemporaneousness. The three, or seven, or fifteen, or seventeen, or eighteen hundred years which have elapsed since his death do not make the least difference, one way or the other. They neither change him, nor reveal, either, who he was; for his real nature is revealed only to faith.

Christ, let me say so with the utmost seriousness, is not an actor; neither is he a merely historical personage since, being the paradox, he is an extremely unhistorical personage. But precisely this is the difference between poetry and reality: contemporaneousness.[1] The difference between poetry and history is no doubt this, that history is what has really happened, and poetry, what is possible, the action which is supposed to have taken place, the life which has taken form in the poet's imagination. But that which really happened (the past) is not necessarily reality, except in a certain sense, viz., in contrast with poetry. There is still lacking in it the criterion of truth (as inwardness) and of all religion, there is still lacking the criterion: the truth FOR YOU. That which is past is not a reality-for me, but only my time is. That which you are contemporaneous with, that is reality-for you. Thus every person has the choice to be contemporaneous with the age in which he is living-and also with one other period, with that of Christ's life here on earth; for Christ's life on earth, or Sacred History, stands by itself, outside of history.

History you may read and hear about as a matter of the past. Within its realm you can, if you so care, judge actions by their results. But in Christ's life here on earth there is nothing past. It did not wait for the assistance of any subsequent results in its own time, 1800 years ago; neither does it now. Historic Christianity is sheer moonshine and

---

[1] As my friend, H. M. Jones, points out, the following passage is essentially Aristotellian: "The true difference is that one (history) relates what has happened, the other (poetry) what may happen"; Poetics," Chap. IX.

un-Christian muddle-headedness. For those true Christians who in every generation live a life contemporaneous with that of Christ have nothing whatsoever to do with Christians of the preceding generation, but all the more with their contemporary, Christ. His life here on earth attends every generation, and every generation severally, as Sacred History; his life on earth is eternal contemporaneousness. For this reason all learned lecturing about Christianity, which has its haunt and hiding-place in the assumption that Christianity is something which belongs to the past and to the 1800 years of history, this lecturing is the most unChristian of heresies, as everyone would readily recognize if he but tried to imagine the generation contemporaneous with Christ as-lecturing! No, we must ever keep in mind that every generation (of the faithful) is contemporaneous with him.

If you cannot master yourself so as to make yourself contemporaneous with him and thus become a Christian; or if he cannot, as your contemporary, draw you to himself, then you will never be a Christian. You may, if you please honor, praise, thank, and with all worldly goods reward him who deludes you into thinking that you are a Christian; nevertheless-he deceives you. You may count yourself happy that you were not contemporaneous with one who dared to assert this; or you may be exasperated to madness by the torment, like that of the gadfly,[1] of being contemporaneous with one who says this to your face: in the first case you are deceived, whereas in the second you have least had a chance to hear the truth.

If you cannot bear this contemporaneousness, and not bear to see this sight in reality-if you cannot prevail upon yourself to go out into the street-and behold! it is God in that loathsome procession; and if you cannot bear to think that this will be your condition also if you kneel and worship him: then you are not essentially a Christian. In that case, what you will have to do is to admit the fact unconditionally to yourself, so that you may, above all, preserve humility, and fear and trembling, when contemplating what it means really to be a Christian. For that way you must proceed, in order to learn and to practice how to flee to grace, so that you will not seek it in vain; but do not, for God's sake, go to any one to be "consoled." For to be sure it is written:

---

[1] Cf. Plato's "Apologia" where Socrates is made to say of himself that he is inflicted on the Athenians like a gadfly on a horse, in order to keep them awake.

"blessed are the eyes which see the things that ye see,"[1] which word the priests have on the tips of their tongues-curiously enough; at times, perhaps, even to defend a worldly finery which, if contemporary with Christ, would be rather incongruous-as if these words had not been said solely about those contemporaries of his who believed. If his exaltation had been evident to the eyes so that everyone without any trouble could have beheld it, why then it would be incorrect to say that Christ abased himself and assumed the guise of a servant, and it would be superfluous to warn against being offended in him; for why in the world should one take offense in an exalted one arrayed in glory? And how in the world will you explain it that Christ fared so ill and that everybody failed to rush up admiringly to behold what was so plain? Ah no, "he hath no form nor comeliness; and when we shall see him, there is no beauty that we should desire him" (Isaiah 53, 2*) [*Kierkegaard's own note.] ; and there was to all appearances nothing remarkable about him who in lowly guise, and by performing signs and wonders, constantly presented the possibility of offense, who claimed to be God-in lowly guise; which therefore expresses: in the first place, what God means by compassion, and by one's self needing to be humble and poor if one wishes to be compassionate; and in the second place, what God means by the misery of mankind. Which, again, in both instances is extremely different from what men mean by these things and which every generation, to the end of time, has to learn over again from the beginning, and beginning in every respect at the same point where those who were contemporary with Christ had to start; that is, to practice these things as contemporaries of Christ. Human impatience and unruliness is, of course, of no avail whatsoever. No man will be able to tell you in how far you may succeed in becoming essentially a Christian. But neither will anxiety and fear and despair help one. Sincerity toward God is the first and the last condition, sincerity in confessing to one's self just where one stands, sincerity before God in ever aiming at one's task. However slowly one may proceed, and if it be but crawling-one is, at any rate, in the right position and is not misled and deceived by the trick of changing the nature of Christ who, instead of being God, is thereby made to represent that sentimental compassion which is man's own invention; by which men, instead of being lifted up to heaven by Christianity, are delayed on their way and remain human and no more.

---

[1] Luke 10,23.

THE MORAL

"And what, then, does all this signify?" It signifies that every one, in silent inwardness before God, is to feel humility before what it means to be in the strictest sense a Christian; is to confess sincerely before God what his position is, so that he may worthily partake of the grace which is offered to everyone who is not perfect, that is, to everyone. And it means no more than that. For the rest let him attend to his work and find joy in it, let him love his wife, rejoicing in her, let him raise his children to be a joy to him, and let him love his fellow-men and enjoy life. God will surely let him know if more is demanded of him, and will also help him to accomplish it; for in the terrifying language of the law this sounds so terrible because it would seem as if man by his own strength were to hold fast to Christ, whereas in the language of love it is Christ that holds fast to him. As was said, then, God will surely let him know if more is demanded of him. But what is demanded of every one is that he humble himself in the presence of God under the demands of ideality. And therefore these demands should be heard, and heard again and again in all their absoluteness. To be a Christian has become a matter of no importance whatever-a mummery, something one is anyway, or something one acquires more readily than a trick. In very truth, it is high time that the demands of ideality were heard.

"But if being a Christian is something so terrifying and awesome, how in all the world can a man get it into his head to wish to accept Christianity?" Very simply and, if you so wish, quite according to Luther: only the consciousness of sin, if I may express myself so, can force one -from the other side, grace exerts the attraction-can force one into this terror. And in the same instant the Christian ideal is transformed, and is sheer mildness, grace, love, and pity. Looking at it any other way, however, Christianity is, and shall ever be, the greatest absurdity, or else the greatest terror. Approach is had only through the consciousness of sin, and to desire to enter by any other way amounts to a crime of lèse-majesté against Christianity.

But sin, or the fact that you and I, individually, are sinners, has at present either been done away with, or else the demands have been lowered in an unjustifiable manner. both in life-the domestic, the civic, as well as the ecclesiastic-and in science which has invented the new doctrine of sin in general. As an equivalent, one has hit upon the device of helping men into Christianity, and keeping them in it, by the aid of a knowledge of world-historic events, of that mild teaching, the exalted and profound spirit of it, about Christ as a friend, etc., etc.-all of which Luther would have called stuff and nonsense and which is really blasphemy, aiming as it does at fraternizing impudently with God and with Christ.

Only the consciousness of being a sinner can inspire one with absolute respect for Christianity. And just because Christianity demands absolute respect it must and shall, to any other way of looking at it, seem absurdity or terror; just because only thereby can the qualitative and absolute emphasis fall on the fact that it is only the consciousness of being a sinner which will procure entrance into it, and at the same time give the vision which, being absolute respect, enables one to see the mildness and love and compassion of Christianity.

The poor in spirit who acknowledge themselves to be sinners, they do not need to know the least thing about the difficulties which appear when one is neither simple nor humble-minded. But when this humble consciousness of one's self, i. e., the individual's, being a sinner is lacking-aye, even though one possessed all human ingenuity and wisdom, and had all accomplishments Possible to man: it will profit him little. Christianity will in the same degree rise terrifying before him and transform itself into absurdity or terror; until he learns, either to renounce it, or else, by the help of what is nothing less than scientific propædeutics, apologetics, etc., that is, through the torments of a contrite heart, to enter into Christianity by the narrow path, through the consciousness of sin.

Selections from 'The Present Moment'[1]

BY WAY OF INTRODUCTION

(No. I, 1)

Plato says somewhere in his "Republic" that things will go well only when those men shall govern the state who do not desire to govern. The idea is probably that, assuming the necessary capability, a man's reluctance to govern affords a good guarantee that he will govern well and efficiently; whereas a man desirous of governing may very easily either abuse his power and become a tyrant, or by his desire to govern be brought into an unforeseen situation of dependence on the people he is to rule, so that his government really becomes an illusion.

This observation applies also to other relations where much depends on taking things seriously: assuming there is ability in a man, it is best that he show reluctance to meddle with them. To be sure, as the proverb has it: "where there is a will there is a way"; but true seriousness appears only when a man fully equal to his task is forced, against his will, to undertake it-against his will, but fully equal to the task.

In this sense I may say of myself that I bear a correct relation to the task in hand: to work in the present moment; for God knows that nothing is more distasteful to me.

Authorship-well, I confess that I find it pleasant; and I may as well admit that I have dearly loved to write-in the manner, to be sure, which suits me. And what I have loved to do is precisely the opposite of

---

[1] Selections.

working in the present moment. What I have loved is precisely remoteness from the present moment-that remoteness in which, like a lover, I may dwell on my thoughts and, like an artist in love with his instrument, entertain myself with language and lure from it the expressions demanded by my thoughts-ah blissful entertainment! In an eternity I should not weary of this occupation.

To contend with men-well, I do like it in a certain sense; for I have by nature a temperament so polemic that I feel in my element only when surrounded by men's mediocrity and meanness. But only on one condition, viz., that I be permitted to scorn them in silence and to satisfy the master passion of my soul: scorn-opportunity for which my career as an author has often enough given me.

I am therefore a man of whom it may be said truthfully that he is not in the least desirous to work in the present moment-very probably I have been called to do so for that very reason.

Now that I am to work in the present moment I must, alas! say farewell to thee, beloved remoteness, where there was no necessity to hurry, but always plenty of time, where I could wait for hours and days and weeks for the proper expression to occur to me; whereas now I must break with all such regards of tender love . [1]And now that I am to work in the present moment I find that there will be not a few persons whom I must oblige by paying my respects to all the insignificant things which mediocrity with great self-importance will lecture about; to all the nonsense which mediocre people, by interpreting into my words their own mediocrity, will find in all I shall write; and to all the lies and calumnies to which a man is exposed against whom those two great powers in society: envy and stupidity, must of necessity conspire.

Why, then, do I wish to work in the present moment? Because I should forever repent of not having done so, and forever repent of having been discouraged by the consideration that the generation now living would find a representation of the essential truths of Christianity interesting and curious reading, at most; having accomplished which they will calmly remain where they are; that is, in the illusion that they are Christians and that the clergy's toying with Christianity really is Christianity.

---

[1] The following sentence is not clear in the original.

A PANEGYRIC ON THE HUMAN RACE OR PROOF THAT THE NEW TESTAMENT IS NO LONGER TRUE

(No. 11, 5)

In the New Testament the Savior of the World, our Lord Jesus Christ, represents the matter in this way: "Strait is the gate, and narrow is the way, which leadeth unto life, and few there be that find it.[1]"

-now, however, just to confine ourselves to Denmark, the way is as broad as a road can possibly be; in fact, the broadest in Denmark, for it is the road we all travel. At the same time it is in all respects a comfortable way, and the gate as wide as it is possible for a gate to be; for certainly a gate cannot be wider than to let all men pass through en masse:

therefore, the New Testament is no longer true '.

All credit is due to the human race! For thou, oh Savior of the World, thou didst entertain too low an estimate of the human race, so that thou didst not foresee the exalted plan which, in its perfectibility, it may reach by steadily continued endeavor!

To such an extent, then, is the New Testament no longer true: the way is the broadest possible, the gate the widest possible, and we are all Christians. In fact, I may venture still further-I am enthusiastic about it, for you see I am writing a panegyric on the human race-I venture to assert that the average Jew living among us is, to a certain degree, a Christian just as well as we others: to such an extent are we all Christians, and to such an extent is the New Testament no longer true.

And, since the point is to find out all which may be adduced to extol the human race, one ought-while having a care not to mention anything which is not true-one ought to watch that nothing, nothing escape one which in this connection may serve as a proof or even as a suggestion. So I venture still further-without wishing to be too positive, as I lack definite information on this subject and would like, therefore, to refer the matter to specialists in this line to decide-: whether there are not present among our domestic animals, or at any rate the nobler ones, such as the horse, the dog, and the cow, indica-

---

[1] Matthew 7, 14.

tions of a Christian spirit. It is not improbable. Consider what it means to live in a Christian state, among a Christian people, where everything is Christian and everybody is a Christian and where one, turn where one may, sees nothing but Christians and Christianity, truth and martyrs for the truth-it is not at all unlikely that this exerts an influence on the nobler domestic animals and thereby again-which is ever of the utmost importance, according to the opinion both of veterinarians and of clergymen-an influence on their progeny. We have all read of Jacob's ruse, how in order to obtain spotted lambs he put party-colored twigs into the watering troughs, so that the ewes saw nothing but mottled things and then brought forth spotted lambs. Hence it is not improbable-although I do not wish to be positive, since I do not belong to the profession, but would rather have this passed on by a committee composed of both clergymen and veterinarians-I say, it is not improbable that the result will finally be that the domestic animals living in a Christian nation will produce a Christian progeny. The thought almost takes away my breath. To be sure, in that case the New Testament will to the greatest possible extent have ceased to be true.

Ah, Thou Savior of the World, when Thou saidst with great concern: "When the Son of man cometh, shall He find Faith on the earth?"[1]-and when Thou didst bow Thy head in death, then didst Thou least of all think that Thy expectations were to be exceeded to such a degree, and that the human race would in such a pretty and touching way render the New Testament no longer true, and Thy significance almost doubtful; for such nice creatures certainly also needed a Savior![2]

---

[1] Luke 18, 8.
[2] The last line of this piece of bloody irony is not clear in the original (S. V. XIII, 128). It will make better sense if one substitutes "da" for the first "de."

Selected Essays

IF WE ARE REALLY CHRISTIANS - THEN WHAT IS GOD?

(No. 11, 8)

If it is not so-that all we mean by being "Christians" is a delusion-that all this machinery, with a State Church and thousands of spiritual-worldly councillors of chancery, etc., is a stupendous delusion which will not be of the least help to us in the life everlasting but, on the contrary, will be turned into an accusation against us-if this is not so; for if it is, then let us, for the sake of life everlasting, get rid of it, the sooner the better-

if it is not so, and if what we understand by being a Christian really is to be a Christian: then what is God in Heaven?

He is the most ridiculous being that ever existed, His Word is the most ridiculous book which has ever appeared; for to move heaven and earth, as He does in his Word, and to threaten with hell and everlasting damnation-in order to obtain as His result what we understand by being Christians (and our assumption was that we a r e true Christians)-well, now, has anything so ridiculous ever been seen before? Imagine that a fellow with a loaded pistol in his hand held up a person and said to him, "I shall shoot you"; or imagine, what is still more terrible, that he said, "I shall seize you and torture you to death in the most horrible manner, if"-now watch, here's the point-"if you do not render your life here on earth as profitable and as enjoyable as you can": would not that be utterly ridiculous? For to obtain that effect it certainly is not necessary to threaten one with a loaded pistol and the most painful torture; in fact, it is possible that neither the loaded pistol nor the most painful torture would be able to deter him from making his life as comfortable as he can. And the same is true when, by fear of eternal punishment (terrible threat!), and by hope of eternal salvation, He wishes to bring about-well, to make us what we a r e (for what we call Christian is, as we have seen, really being Christian), to make us-well, to make us what we are; that is, make men live as they please; for to abstain from committing crimes is nothing but common prudence!

The most terrible blasphemy is the one of which "Christianity" is guilty, which is, to transform the God of the Spirit into-a ridiculous piece of nonsense. And the stupidest kind of worship, more stupid than any idolatry ever was among the heathen, and more stupid than to worship as a god some stone, or an ox, or an insect-more stupid than anything, is to adore as god-a fool!

DIAGNOSIS

(No. IV, 1)

1.

Every physician will admit that by the correct diagnosis of a malady more than half the fight against it is won; also, that if a correct diagnosis has not been made, all skill and all care and attention will be of little avail.

The same is true with regard to religion.

We are agreed to let stand the claim that in "Christendom" we are Christians, every one of us; and then we have laid and, perhaps, will lay, emphasis now on this, now on that, side of the teachings of the Scriptures.

But the truth is: we are not only not Christians-no, we are not even the heathen to whom Christianity may be taught without misgivings, and what is worse, we are prevented through a delusion, an enormous delusion (viz. "Christendom," the Christian state, a Christian country, a Christian world) from becoming Christians.

And then the suggestion is made to one to continue untouched and unchanged this delusion and, rather, to furnish a new presentation of the teachings of Christ.[1]

This has been suggested; and, in a certain sense, it is altogether fitting. Just because one lives in a delusion (not to speak even of being interested in keeping up the delusion), one is bound to desire that which will feed the malady-a common enough observation this-the sick man desiring precisely those things which feed his malady.

2.

Imagine a hospital. The patients are dying off like so many flies. The methods are changed, now this way, now that: of no avail! What may be the cause? The cause lies in the building-the whole building is tainted. The patients are put down as having died, the one of this, the other of that, disease, but strictly speaking this is not true; for they all died from the taint which is in the building.

---

[1] This suggestion had actually been made to Kierkegaard in the course of his attacks on Martensen.

The same is true in religion. That religious conditions are wretched, and that people in respect of their religion are in a wretched condition, nothing is more certain. So one ventures the opinion that if we could but have a new hymn-book; and another, if we could but have a new service-book; and a third, if we could but have a musical service, etc., etc.-that then matters would mend.

In vain; for the fault lies in the edifice. The whole ramshackle pile of a State Church which has not been aired, spiritually speaking, in times out of mind-the air in it has developed a taint. And therefore religious life has become diseased or has died out; alas, for precisely that which the worldly mind regards as health is, in a Christian sense, disease-just as, vice versa, that which is healthy in a Christian sense, is regarded as diseased from a worldly point of view.

Then let the ramshackle pile collapse, get it out of the way, close all these shops and booths which are the only ones which are excepted from the strict Sunday regulations, forbid this official double-dealing, put them out of commission, and provide for them, for all these quacks: even though it is true that the royally attested physician is the acceptable one, and he who is not so attested is a quack: in Christianity it is just the reverse; that is, the royally attested teacher is the quack, is a quack by the very fact that he is royally attested-and let us worship God again in simplicity, instead of making a fool of him in splendid edifices; let us be in earnest again and stop playing; for a Christianity preached by royal officials who are payed and insured by the state and who use the police against the others, such a Christianity bears about the same relation to the Christianity of the New Testament as swimming with the help of a cork-belt or a bladder does to swimming alone-it is mere play.

Yes, let that come about. What Christianity needs is not the stifling protection of the state-ah no, it needs fresh air, it needs persecution and-the protection of God. The state does only mischief in averting persecution and surely is not the medium through which God's protection can be conducted. Whatever you do, save Christianity from the state, for with its protection it overlies Christianity like a fat woman overlying her child with her carcass, beside teaching Christianity the most abominable bad habits-as, e.g., to use the police force and to call that Christianity.

3.

A person is growing thinner every day and is wasting away. What may the trouble be? For surely he is not suffering want! "No, sure enough," says the doctor, "that is not the trouble. The trouble is precisely with his eating, with his eating in season and out of season, with his eating without being hungry, with his using stimulants to produce an appetite, and in this manner ruining his digestion, so that he is wasting away as if he suffered want." The same is true in religion. The worst of all is to satisfy a craving which has not as yet made its appearance, to anticipate it, or-worse still-by the help of stimulants to produce something which looks like a craving, which then is promptly satisfied. Ah, the shame of it! And yet this is exactly what is being done in religion where people are in very truth fooled out of the real meaning of life and helped to waste their lives. That is in very truth, the effect of this whole machinery of a state church and a thousand royal officials who, under the pretense of being spiritual guides for the people, trick them out of the highest thing in life, which is, the solicitude about one's self, and the need which would surely of itself find a teacher or minister after its own mind; whereas now the need-and it is just the growth of this sense of a need which gives life its highest significance-whereas now this need does not arise at all, but on the contrary is forestalled by being satisfied long before it can arise. And this is the way, they claim, this is the way to continue the work which the Savior of Mankind did begin-stunting the human race as they do. And why is this so? Because there happen to be a thousand and one royal officials who have to support their families by furnishing what is called-spiritual guidance for men's souls!

Søren Kierkegaard

THE CHRISTIANITY OF THE NEW TESTAMENT;

THE CHRISTANITY OF "CHRISTENDOM"

(No. V, 4)

The intention of Christianity was: to change everything.

The result, the Christianity of "Christendom" is: everything, literally everything, remained as it had been, with just the difference that to everything was affixed the attribute "Christian"-and for the rest (strike up, fiddlers!) we live in Heathendom-so merrily, so merrily the dance goes around; or, rather, we live in a Heathendom made more refined by the help of Life Everlasting and by help of the thought that, after all, it is all Christian!

Try it, point to what you will, and you shall see that I am right in my assertion.

If what Christianity demanded was chastity, then away with brothels! But the change is that the brothels have remained just as they did in Heathendom, and the proportion of prostitutes remained the same, too; to be sure, they became "Christian" brothels! A brothel-keeper is a "Christian" brothel-keeper, he is a Christian as well as we others. Exclude him from church membership? "Why, for goodness sake," the clergyman will say, "what would things come to if we excluded a single paying member?" The brothel-keeper dies and gets a funeral oration with a panegyric in proportion to the amount he pays. And after having earned his money in a manner which, from a Christian point of view, is as filthy and base as can be (for, from a Christian point of view it would be more honorable if he had stolen it) the clergyman returns home. He is in a hurry, for he is to go to church in order to deliver an oration or, as Bishop Martensen would say, "bear witness."

But if Christianity demanded honesty and uprightness, and doing away with this swindle, the change which really came about was this: the swindling has remained just as in Heathendom, "every one (every Christian) is a thief in his own line"; only, the swindling has taken on the predicate "Christian." So we now have "Christian" swindling-and the "clergyman" bestows his blessing on this Christian community, this Christian state, in which one cheats just as one did in Heathendom, at the same time that one pays the "clergyman," that is, the biggest swindler of them all, and thus cheats one's self into Christianity.

And if Christianity demanded seriousness in life and doing away with the praise and approbation of vanity-why, everything has remained as before, with just this difference that it has assumed the predicate "Christian." Thus the trumpery business with decorations, titles, and rank, etc. has become Christian-and the clergyman (that most decent of all indecencies, that most ridiculous of all ridiculous hodge-podges), he is as pleased as Punch to be decorated himself-with the "cross." The cross? Why, certainly; for in the Christianity of "Christendom" has not the cross become something like a child's hobby-horse and tin-trumpet?

And so with everything. There is implanted in man no stronger instinct, after that of self-preservation, than the instinct of reproduction; for which reason Christianity seeks to reduce its strength, teaching that it is better not to marry; "but if they cannot contain, let them marry; for it better to marry than to burn." But in Christendom the propagation of the race has become the serious business of life and of Christianity; and the clergyman-that quintessence of nonsense done up in long clothes-the clergyman, the teacher of Christianity, of the Christianity of the New Testament, has his income adjusted to the fact that the human race is active in propagating the race, and gets a little something for each child!

As I said, look about you and you will find that everything is as I told you: the change from Heathendom consists in everything remaining unchanged but having assumed the predicate "Christian."

Søren Kierkegaard

MODERN RELIGIOUS GUARANTEES

(No. V, 8)

In times long, long past people looked at matters in this fashion: it was demanded of him who would be a teacher of Christianity that his life should be a guarantee for the teachings he proclaimed.

This idea was abandoned long ago, the world having become wiser and more serious. It has learned to set little store by these illiberal and sickly notions of personal responsibility, having learned to look for purely objective ends. The demand is made now of the teacher that his life should guarantee that what he has to say is entertaining and dramatic stuff, amusing, and purely objective.

Some examples. Suppose you wanted to speak about Christianity, that is, the Christianity of the New Testament which expresses preference for the single state-and suppose you yourself are unmarried: why, my dear man! you ought not to speak on this subject, because your congregation might think that you meant what you said and become disquieted, or it might feel insulted that you thus, very improperly, mixed in your own affairs. No, dear sir, it will take a little longer before you are entitled to speak seriously on this matter so as really to satisfy the congregation. Wait till you have buried your first wife and are well along with your second wife: then it will be time for you to stand before your congregation to preach and "bear witness" that Christianity prefers the single state-then you will satisfy them altogether; for your life will furnish the guarantee that it is all tomfoolery and great fun, or that what you say is-interesting. Indeed, how interesting! For just as, to make it interesting, the husband must be unfaithful to his wife and the wife to her husband, likewise truth becomes interesting, intensely interesting, only when one lets one's self be carried away by one's feelings, be fascinated by them-but of course does the precise opposite and thus in an underhand manner is re-assured in persisting in one's ways.

Do you wish to speak about Christianity's teaching contempt for titles and decorations and all the follies of fame-and should you happen to be neither a person of rank nor anything of the kind: Why, my dear sir! You ought not to undertake to speak on this subject. Why, your congregation might think you were in earnest, or feel insulted by such a lack of tact in forcing your personality on their notice. No, indeed, you ought to wait till you have a lot of decorations, the more the merrier; you ought to wait till you drag along with a rigmarole of titles, so many that you hardly know yourself what you are called: then is your time come to stand before your congregation to preach and "bear witness"-and you will undoubtedly satisfy them; for your life will then furnish the guarantee that it is but a dramatic divertissement, an interesting forenoon entertainment.

Is it your intention to preach Christianity in poverty, and insist that only thus it is taught in truth-and you happen to be very literally a poor devil: Why, my dear sir! You ought not to venture to speak on this subject. Why, your congregation might think you were in earnest, they might become afraid and lose their good humor, and they might be very unpleasantly affected by thus having poverty thrust in on them. No indeed, first get yourself some fat living, and when you have had it so long that your promotion to one still fatter is to be expected: then is your time come to stand before your congregation and to preach and "bear witness"-and you will satisfy them; for your life then furnishes the guarantee that it is just a joke, such as serious men like to indulge in, now and then, in theatre or in church, as a sort of recreation to gather new strength for making money.

And that is the way they honor God in the churches! And then these silk and velvet orators weep, they sob, their voice is drowned in tears! Ah, if it be true (and it is, since God Himself has said so), if it be true that He counts the tears of the afflicted and puts them into His bottle,[1] then woe to these orators, if God has counted also their Sunday tears and put them into His bottle! And woe to us all if God really heeds these Sunday tears-especially those of the speakers, but also those of the listeners! For a Sunday preacher would indeed be right if he said-and, oratorically, this would have a splendid effect, especially if accompanied by his own tears and suppressed sobs-he would be right if he said to his audience: I shall count all the futile tears you have shed in church, and with them I shall step accusingly before you on the Day of Judgment-indeed, he is right; only please not to forget that, after all, the speaker's own dramatic tears are by far more dreadful than the thoughtless tears of his listeners.

---

[1] Allusion to Psalm 56, 9; also to a passage in one of Bishop Mynster's sermons (S. V.).

Søren Kierkegaard

WHAT SAYS THE FIRE-MARSHAL

(No. VI, 5)

That a man who in some fashion or other has what one calls a "cause," something he seriously purposes to accomplish-and there are other persons who make it their business to counteract, and antagonize, and hurt him-that he must take measures against these his enemies, this will be evident to everyone. But that there is a well-intentioned kindness by far more dangerous, perhaps, and one that seems calculated to prevent the serious accomplishment of his mission, this will not at once be clear to everyone.

When a person suddenly falls ill, kindly-intentioned folk will straightway rush to his help, and one will suggest this, another that-and if all those about him had a chance to have their way it would certainly result in the sick man's death; seeing that even one person's well-meaning advice may be dangerous enough. And even if nothing is done, and the advice of neither the assembled and well-meaning crowd nor of any one person is taken, yet their busy and flurried presence may be harmful, nevertheless, inasmuch as they are in the way of the physician.

Likewise at a fire. Scarcely has the alarm of fire been sounded but a great crowd of people will rush to the spot, good and kindly and sympathetic, helpful people, the one with a bucket, the other with a basin, still another with a hand-squirt-all of them goodly, kindly, sympathetic, helpful persons who want to do all they can to extinguish the fire.

But what says the fire-marshal? The fire-marshal, he says-well, at other times the fire-marshal is a very pleasant and refined man; but at a fire he does use coarse language-he says or, rather, he roars out: "Oh, go to hell with your buckets and hand-squirts!" And then, when these well-meaning people feel insulted, perhaps, and think it highly improper to be treated in this fashion, and would like at least to be treated respectfully-what says the fire-marshal then? Well, at other times the fire-marshal is a very pleasant and refined gentleman who will show every one the respect due him; but at a fire he is somewhat different-he says: "Where the devil is the police?" And when the policemen arrive he says to them: "Rid me of these damn people with their buckets and hand-squirts; and if they won't clear out, then club them on their heads, so that we get rid of them and-can get at the fire!"

That is to say, in the case of a fire the whole way of looking at things is a very different one from that of quiet every-day life. The qualities which in quiet every-day life render one well-liked, viz., good-nature and kindly well m-eaning, all this is repaid, in the case of a fire, with abusive language and finally with a crack on the head.

And this is just as it should be. For a conflagration is a serious business; and wherever we have to deal with a se-rious business this well-intentioned kindness won't do at all. Indeed, any serious business enforces a very different mode of behavior which is: either-or. Either you are able really to do something, and really have something to do here; or else, if that be not the case, then the serious business demands precisely that you take yourself away. And if you will not comprehend that, the fire-marshal proposes to have the police hammer it into your head; which may do you a great deal of good, as it may help to render you a little serious, as is befitting so serious a business as a fire.

But what is true in the case of a fire holds true also in matters of the spirit. Wherever a cause is to be promoted, or an enterprise to be seen through, or an idea to be served -you may be sure that when he who really is the man to do it, the right man, he who, in a higher sense has and ought to have command, he who is in earnest and can make the matter the serious business it really is-you may be sure that when he arrives at the spot, so to say, he will find there a nice company of easy-going, addle-pated twaddlers who, pretending to be engaged in serious business, dabble in wishing to serve this cause, to further that enterprise, to promote that idea-a company of addle-pated fools who will of course consider one's unwillingness to make common cause with them (which unwillingness precisely proves one's seriousness) - will of course consider that a sure proof of the man's lack of serious-ness. I say, when the right man arrives he will find this; but I might also look at it in this fashion: the very question as to whether he is the right man is most properly decided by his attitude to that crowd of fools. If he thinks they may help him, and that he will add to his strength by joining them, then he is eo ipso not the right man. The right man will understand at once, as did the fire-marshal, that the crowd must be got out of the way; in fact, that their presence and put-tering around is the most dangerous ally the fire could have. Only, that in matters of the spirit it is not as in the case of the conflagration, where the fire-marshal needs but to say to the police: rid me of these people!

Thus in matters of the spirit, and likewise in matters of religion. History has frequently been compared to what the chemists call a "process." The figure is quite suggestive, providing it is correctly understood. For instance, in the "process of filtration" water is run through a filter and by this process loses its impurities. In a totally different sense history is a process. The idea is given utterance-and then enters into the process of history. But unfortunately this process (how ridiculous a supposition!) consists not in purifying the idea, which never is purer than at its inception; oh no, it consists in gradually and increasingly botching, bungling, and making a mess of, the idea, in using up the idea, in-indeed, is not this the opposite of filtering?- adding the impurer elements which it originally lacked: until at last, by the enthusiastic and mutually appreciative efforts of successive generations, the idea has absolutely disappeared and the very opposite of the original idea is now called the idea, which is then asserted to have arisen through a historic process by which the idea is purified and elevated.

When finally the right man arrives, he who in the highest sense is called to the task-for all we know, chosen early and slowly educated for this business-which is, to throw light on the matter, to set fire to this jungle which is a refuge for all kinds of foolish talk and delusions and rascally tricks-when he comes he will always find a nice company of addle-pated fools and twaddlers who, surely enough, do think that, perhaps, things are wrong and that "something must be done about it"; or who have taken the position, and talk a good deal about it, that it is preposterous to be self-important and talk about it. Now if he, the right man, is deceived but a single instant and thinks that it is this company who are to aid him, then it is clear he is not the right man. If he is deceived and has dealings with that company, then providence will at once take its hand off him, as not fit. But the right man will see at a glance, as the fire-marshal does, that the crowd who in the kindness of their hearts mean to help in extinguishing a conflagration by buckets and hand-squirts-the right man will see that the same crowd who here, when there is a question, not of extinguishing a fire, but rather of setting something on fire, will in the kindness of their hearts wish to help with a sulphur match sans fire or a wet spill-he will see that this crowd must be got rid of, that he must not have the least thing in common with this crowd, that he will be obliged to use the coarsest possible language against them-he who perhaps at other times is anything but coarse. But the thing of supreme importance is to be rid of the crowd; for the effect of the crowd is to hamstring the whole cause by robbing it of its seriousness while heartfelt sympathy is pretended. Of course the crowd will then rage against him, against his incredible arrogance and so forth. This ought not to count with him, whether for or against, In all truly serious business the law of : either-or, prevails. Either, I am the man whose serious business this is, I am called to it, and am willing to take a decisive risk; or, if this be not the case, then the seriousness of the business demands that I do not meddle with it at all. Nothing is more detestable and mean, and nothing discloses and effects a deeper demoralization, than this lackadaisical wishing to enter "somewhat" into matters which demand an aut-aut, aut Caesar aut nihil,[1] this taking just a little part in something, to be so wretchedly lukewarm, to twaddle about the business, and then by twaddling to usurp through a lie the attitude of being better than they who wish not to have anything whatever to do with the whole business-to usurp through a lie the attitude of being better, and thus to render doubly difficult the task of him whose business it really is.

---

[1] Either-or; either Cæsar or nothing (Cæsare Borgia's slogan).

Søren Kierkegaard

CONFIRMATION AND WEDDING CEREMONY; CHRISTIAN COMEDY-OR WORSE STILL

(No. VII, 6)

Pricks of conscience (insofar as they may be assumed in this connection)-pricks of conscience seem to have convinced "Christendom" that it was, after all, going too far, and that it would not do-this beastly farce of becoming a Christian by the simple method of letting a royal official give the infant a sprinkle of water over his head, which is the occasion for a family gathering with a banquet to celebrate the day.

This won't do, was the opinion of "Christendom," for the opportunity ought to be given the baptized individual to indorse personally his baptismal vows.

For this purpose the rite of confirmation was devised-a splendid invention, providing we take two things for granted: in the first place, that the idea of divine worship is to make God ridiculous; and in the second place, that its purpose is to give occasion for family celebrations, parties, a jolly evening, a banquet which is different from other banquets in that it-ah, exquisite-in that it, "at the same time" has a religious significance.

"The tender child," thus Christendom, "can of course not assume the baptismal vow personally, for this requires a real personality." Consequently there was chosen-is this a stroke of genius or just ingenious?-there was chosen the age of 14 or 15 years, the schoolboy age. This real personality-that is all right, if you please-he is equal to the task of personally assuming responsibility for the baptismal vow taken in behalf of the infant.

A boy of fifteen! Now, if it were a matter of 10 dollars, his father would probably say: "No, my boy, I can't let you have all that money, you are still too green for that." But for a matter touching his eternal salvation where the point is to assume, with all the seriousness one's personality is capable of, and as a personality, responsibility for what certainly could not in any profounder sense be called serious-when a child is bound by a vow: for that the age of fifteen is excellently fitting.

Excellently fitting. Oh yes if, as was remarked above, divine worship serves a double purpose, viz., to render God ridiculous in a very adroit manner-if you may call it so-and to furnish the occasion for graceful family celebrations. In that case it is indeed excellently fitting, as everything is on that occasion; as is, likewise, the customary biblical lesson for the day which, you will remember, begins: "Then the same day at evening, when the doors were shut"[1]-and this text is particularly suitable to a Confirmation Sunday. One is truly edified when hearing a clergyman read it on a Confirmation Sunday.

As is easily perceived, then, the confirmation ceremony is still worse nonsense than the baptism of infants, just because confirmation pretends to supply what was lacking at the baptism, viz., a real personality capable of making a vow in a matter touching one's eternal salvation. In another sense this nonsense is, to be sure, ingenious enough, as serving the self-interest of the clergy who understand full well that if the decision concerning a man's religion were reserved until he had reached maturity (which were the only Christian, as well as the only sensible, way), many might possess character enough to refuse to become Christians by an act of hypocrisy. For this reason "the clergyman" seeks to gain control of men in their infancy and their youth, so that they would find it difficult, upon reaching a more mature age, to break a "sacred" vow dating, to be sure, from one's boyhood, but which would, perhaps, still be a serious enough matter to many a one. Hence the clergy take hold of the infants, the youths, and receive sacred promises and the like from them. And what that man of God, "the clergyman," does, why, that is, of course, a God-fearing action. Else, analogy might, perhaps, demand that to the ordinance forbidding the sale of spirituous liquors to minors there should be added one forbidding the taking of solemn vows concerning one's eternal salvation from-boys; which ordinance would look toward preventing the clergy, who themselves are perjurers, from working-in order to salve their own consciences-from working toward the greatest conceivable shipwreck which is, to make all society become perjured; for letting boys of fifteen bind themselves in a matter touching their eternal salvation is a measure which is precisely calculated to have that effect.

The ceremony of confirmation is, then, in itself a worse piece of nonsense than the baptism of infants. But in order to miss nothing which might, in any conceivable manner, contribute to render confirmation the exact opposite of what it purports to be, this ceremony has been connected with all manner of worldly and civil affairs, so that the

---

[1] John 20, 19-"Where the disciples were assembled for fear of the Jews, came Jesus and stood in the midst, and saith unto them, Peace be unto you."

significance of confirmation lies chiefly in the-certificate of character which the minister makes out; without which certificate no boy or girl will be able to get on at all in life.[1]

The whole thing is a comedy; and perhaps something might be done to add greater dramatic illusion to the solemnity; as e.g., passing an ordinance forbidding anyone to be confirmed in a jacket, as not becoming a real personality; likewise, a regulation ordering male candidates for confirmation to wear a beard during the ceremony, which beard might, of course, be taken off for the family celebration in the evening, or be used in fun and merrymaking.

I am not now attacking the community-they are led astray; they cannot be blamed for liking this kind of divine worship, seeing that they are left to their own devices and deceived by their clergyman who has sworn an oath on the New Testament. But woe to these clergymen, woe to them, these sworn liars! I know there have been mockers at religion, and I know how much they would have given to be able to do what I do; but they were not able to, because God was not with them. It is different with me. Originally as well disposed to the clergy as few have been, and very ready to help them, I have undergone a change of heart in the opposite direction, owing to their attitude. And the Almighty is with me, and He knows how the whip is to be handled so that the blows take effect, and that laughter must be that whip, handled with fear and trembling-therefor am I used.

---

[1] This was, until very recently, the universal rule in Protestant Scandinavia and Germany.

THE WEDDING CEREMONY

True worship of God consists, very simply, in doing God's will.

But that kind of divine service has never suited man's wishes. That which occupies man's mind at all times, that which gives rise to science[1] and makes science spread into many, many sciences, and into interminable detail; that of which, and for which, thousands of clergymen and professors live, that which forms the contents of the history of Christendom, by the study of which the clergyman or the professor to be is trained-is to get a different kind of worship arranged, the main point of which would be: to do what one pleases, but in such fashion that the name of God and the invocation of God be brought into connection therewith; by which arrangement man imagines himself safeguarded against ungodliness-whereas, alas! just this procedure is the most unqualified ungodliness.

For example: a man has the intention to make his living by killing people. To be sure, he knows from the Word of God that this is not permissible, that God's will is: thou shalt not kill! "All right," thinks he, "but this way of serving God will not serve my purposes-at the same time I don't care to be among the ungodly ones, either." So what does he do but get hold of some priest who in God's name blesses his dagger. Ah, c'est bien autre chose!

In the Scriptures the single state is recommended. "But," says man, "that kind of worship really does not serve my purposes-and surely, you can't say that I am an ungodly person; and such an important step as marriage (which nota bene God counsels against, His opinion being, in fact, that the important thing is not to take "this important step")-should I take such an important step without making sure of God's blessing?" Bravo! "That is what we have the priest for, that man of God, he will bestow the blessing on this important step (nota bene concerning which the most important thing was not to take it at all) and so it will be acceptable to God"-and so I have my own way; and my own way becomes the way of worshipping God; and the priest has his own way and gets his ten dollars, which are not earned in such a simple way as, for example, by brushing people's clothes, or by serving out beer and brandy-oh no! Was he not active on behalf of God? To earn ten dollars in this fashion is: serving God. Bravissimo!

---

[1] It is to be borne in mind that Danish *videnskab*, like German *Wissenschaft*, embraces the humanities and theology as well.

Søren Kierkegaard

What depth of nonsense and abomination! If something is not pleasing to God, does it perhaps become pleasing to Him by having-why, that is aggravating the mischief!-by having a clergyman along who-why, that is aggravating the mischief still more!-who gets ten dollars for declaring it pleasant to God?

Let us consider the marriage ceremony still further! In His word God recommends the single state. Now suppose two young people want to be married. To be sure, they ought certainly to know, themselves, what Christianity is, seeing that they call themselves Christians; but never mind that now. The lovers then apply to-the clergyman; and the clergyman is, we remember, pledged by his oath on the New Testament (which nota bene recommends the single state). Now, if he is not a liar and a perjurer who makes his money in the very shabbiest fashion, he would be bound to take the following course: at most he could, with human compassion for this human condition of being in love, say to them: "Dear children, I am the one to whom you should turn last of all; to turn to me on this occasion is, indeed, as strange as if one should turn to the chief of police and ask him how best to steal. My duty is to employ all means to restrain you. At most, I can say, with the words of the Apostle (for they are not the words of Our Lord), I can say to you: well, if it must be, and you cannot contain, why, then find some way of getting together; for 'it is better to marry than to burn.'[1] I know very well that you will be likely to shudder when I speak in this manner about what you think is the most beautiful thing in life; but I must do my duty. And it is therefore I said to you that to me you should have applied last of all."

It is different in "Christendom." The priest-oh dear me!-if there are but two to clap together, why certainly! Indeed, if the persons concerned turned to a midwife they would perhaps not be as sure to be confirmed in their conviction that their intention is pleasing to God.

And so they are married; i.e. man has his own way, and this having his own way strategically serves at the same time as divine worship, God's name being connected with it. They are married-by the priest! Ah, for having the clergyman along is just what reassures one-the man who, to be sure, is pledged by his oath to preach the New Testament, but who for a consideration of ten dollars is the pleasantest company one could desire-that man he guarantees that this act is true worship of God.

---

[1] I Cor. 7,9.

In a Christian sense one ought to say: precisely the fact that a priest is in it, precisely that is the worst thing about the whole business. If you want to be married you ought, rather, be married by a smith; for then-if it were admissible to speak in this fashion-then it might possibly escape God's attention; whereas, if there is a priest along it can certainly not escape His attention. Precisely the fact of the clergyman's being there makes it as criminal an affair as possible-call to mind what was said to a man who in a storm at sea invoked the gods: "By all means do not let the gods notice that you are aboard!" Thus one might say here also: By all means try to avoid calling in a priest. The others, the smith and the lovers, have not pledged themselves by an oath on the New Testament, so matters are not as bad-if it be admissible to speak in this fashion-as when the priest assists with his-holy presence.

Søren Kierkegaard

AN ETERNITY TO REPENT IN!

(No. VIII, 3)

Let me relate a story. I did not read it in a book of devotion but in what is generally called light reading. Yet I do not hesitate to make use of it, and indicate its source only lest anyone be disturbed if he should happen to be acquainted with it, or find out at some later time where it is from-lest he be disturbed that I had been silent about this.

Once upon a time there lived somewhere in the East a poor old couple. Utterly poor they were, and anxiety about the future naturally grew when they thought of old age approaching. They did not, indeed, constantly assail heaven with their prayers, they were too God-fearing to do that; but still they were ever praying to God for help.

Then one morning it happened that the old woman found an exceeding large jewel on the hearth-stone, which she forthwith showed to her husband, who recognized its value and easily perceived that now their poverty was at an end.

What a bright future for these old people, and what gladness! But frugal and pious as they were they decided not to sell the jewel just yet, since they had enough wherewithal to live still one more day. But on the morrow they would sell it, and then a new life was to begin for them.

In the following night the woman dreamed that she was transported to Paradise. An angel showed her about the splendors which only an Oriental imagination can devise. He showed her a hall in which there stood long rows of arm-chairs gemmed all over with precious stones and pearls. These, so the angel explained, were the seats of the pious. And last of all he pointed out to her the one destined for herself. When regarding it more closely she discovered that a very large jewel was lacking in the back of the chair, and she asked the angel how that might be. He-ah, watch now, for here is the point! The angel answered: "That was the jewel which you found on your hearth-stone. It was given you ahead of time, and it cannot be put in again."

In the morning the woman told her husband this dream. And she was of the opinion that it was better, perhaps, to endure in poverty the few years still left to them to live, rather than to be without that jewel in all eternity. And her pious husband was of the same opinion.

So in the evening they laid the jewel on the hearth-stone and prayed to God to take it away again. And next morning it had disappeared, for certain; and what had become of it the old folks well knew: it was in its right place again.

This man was in truth happily married, and his wife a sensible woman. But even if it were true, as is maintained so often, that it is men's wives who cause them to lose sight of eternal values: even if all men remained unmarried, there would still be in every one of us an impulse, more ingenious and more pressing and more unremitting than a woman, which will cause him to use a wrong measure and to think a couple of years, or ten years, or forty years, so enormous a length of time that even eternity were quite brief in comparison; instead of these years being as nothing when compared with the infinite duration of eternity.

Therefore, heed this well! You may by worldly wisdom escape perhaps what it has pleased God to unite with the condition of one's being a Christian, that is, sufferings and tribulations; you may, and to your own destruction, by cleverly avoiding the difficulties, perhaps, gain what God has forever made incompatible with being a Christian, that is, the enjoyment of pleasures and all earthly goods; you may, fooled by your own worldly wisdom, perhaps, finally perish altogether, in the illusion that you are on the right way because you have gained happiness in this world: and then-you will have an eternity to repent in! An eternity to repent in; to repent that you did not employ your time in doing what might be remembered in all eternity; that is, in truth to love God, with the consequence that you suffer the persecution of men in this life.

Therefore, do not deceive yourself, and of all deceivers fear most yourself! Even if it were possible for one, with regard to eternity, to take something ahead of time, you would still deceive yourself just by having something ahead of time-and then an eternity to repent in!

Søren Kierkegaard

A DOSE OF DISGUST WITH LIFE

(No. IX, 3)

Just as man-as is natural-desires that which tends to nourish and revive his love of life, likewise he who wishes to live with eternity in mind needs a constant dose of disgust with life lest he become foolishly enamored of this world and, still more, in order that he may learn thoroughly to be disgusted and bored and sickened with the folly and lies of this wretched world. Here is a dose of it:

God Incarnate is betrayed, mocked, deserted by absolutely all men; not a single one, literally not a single one, remains faithful to him-and then, afterwards, afterwards,-oh yes, afterwards, there were millions of men who on their knees made pilgrimage to the places where many hundred years ago His feet, perhaps, trod the ground; afterwards, afterwards-oh yes, afterwards, millions worshipped a splinter of the cross on which He was crucified!

And so it was always when men were contemporary with the great; but afterwards, afterwards-oh yes, afterwards!

Must one then not loathe being human?

And again, must one not loathe being human? For these millions who on their knees made pilgrimage to His grave, this throng of people which no power on earth was able to overcome: but one thing were necessary, Christ's return-and all these millions would quickly regain their feet to run their way, so that the whole throng were as if blown away; or would, in a mass, and erect enough, rush upon Christ in order to kill him.

That which Christ and the Apostles and every martyr desires, and desires as the only thing: that we should follow in His footsteps, just that is the thing which mankind does not like or does not find pleasure in.

No, take away the danger-so that it is but play, and then the battalions of the human race will (ah, disgusting!) will perform astonishing feats in aping Him; and then instead of an imitation of Christ we get (ah, disgusting!), we get that sacred buffoonery-under guidance and command (ah, disgusting!) of sworn clergymen who do service as sergeants, lieutenants, etc.-ordained men who therefore have the Holy Spirit's special assistance in this serious business.

Also from Benediction Books ...

"THE KINGDOM OF GOD IS WITHIN YOU"
CHRISTIANITY NOT AS A MYSTIC RELIGION BUT AS A
NEW THEORY OF LIFE
LEO TOLSTOY
Benediction Books, 2011
298 pages
ISBN: 978-1-84902-474-7

Available from www.amazon.com, www.amazon.co.uk

Also from Benediction Books …
Wandering Between Two Worlds: Essays on Faith and Art
Anita Mathias
Benediction Books, 2007
152 pages
ISBN: 0955373700

Available from www.amazon.com, www.amazon.co.uk

In these wide-ranging lyrical essays, Anita Mathias writes, in lush, lovely prose, of her naughty Catholic childhood in Jamshedpur, India; her large, eccentric family in Mangalore, a sea-coast town converted by the Portuguese in the sixteenth century; her rebellion and atheism as a teenager in her Himalayan boarding school, run by German missionary nuns, St. Mary's Convent, Nainital; and her abrupt religious conversion after which she entered Mother Teresa's convent in Calcutta as a novice. Later rich, elegant essays explore the dualities of her life as a writer, mother, and Christian in the United States-- Domesticity and Art, Writing and Prayer, and the experience of being "an alien and stranger" as an immigrant in America, sensing the need for roots.

About the Author

Anita Mathias is the author of *Wandering Between Two Worlds: Essays on Faith and Art*. She has a B.A. and M.A. in English from Somerville College, Oxford University, and an M.A. in Creative Writing from the Ohio State University, USA. Anita won a National Endowment of the Arts fellowship in Creative Nonfiction in 1997. She lives in Oxford, England with her husband, Roy, and her daughters, Zoe and Irene.

Anita's website:
   http://www.anitamathias.com, and
Anita's blog Dreaming Beneath the Spires:
   http://dreamingbeneaththespires.blogspot.com

The Church That Had Too Much
Anita Mathias
Benediction Books, 2010
52 pages
ISBN: 9781849026567

Available from www.amazon.com, www.amazon.co.uk

The Church That Had Too Much was very well-intentioned. She wanted to love God, she wanted to love people, but she was both hampered by her muchness and the abundance of her possessions, and beset by ambition, power struggles and snobbery. Read about the surprising way The Church That Had Too Much began to resolve her problems in this deceptively simple and enchanting fable.

About the Author

Anita Mathias is the author of *Wandering Between Two Worlds: Essays on Faith and Art*. She has a B.A. and M.A. in English from Somerville College, Oxford University, and an M.A. in Creative Writing from the Ohio State University, USA. Anita won a National Endowment of the Arts fellowship in Creative Nonfiction in 1997. She lives in Oxford, England with her husband, Roy, and her daughters, Zoe and Irene.

Anita's website:
    http://www.anitamathias.com, and
Anita's blog Dreaming Beneath the Spires:
    http://dreamingbeneaththespires.blogspot.com

www.ingramcontent.com/pod-product-compliance
Lightning Source LLC
Chambersburg PA
CBHW031352040426
42444CB00005B/260